Hey,
Can I Just
Write?

Hey, Can I Just Write?

JOY DURDEN

Library of Congress Control Number: 2019918101
ISBN: Hardcover   978-1-7960-7040-8
                 Softcover   978-1-7960-7039-2
                 eBook   978-1-7960-7038-5

Rev. date: 11/27/2019

To order additional copies of this book, contact:
Xlibris
1-888-795-4274
www.Xlibris.com
Orders@Xlibris.com
802033

CONTENTS

Books of Wisdom

My Revelations
Short Stories

Poetry, Prose, Creative Writing

Written Verse Messages for the Young

African American Verse/Black History

In Memoriam

About The Book

I am sure you are wondering about the title of my first book, *Hey, Can I Just Write?* Honestly, it was the first and after many considerations, the final title. This title is my way of conveying my creative frustration in a rebellious way. I had no wish to conform to one particular genre at this time and wanted to express so much in so many ways. I simply wanted to write it all out. I needed to put words to my grief, my pain, my loss, my happiness, my life.

This book reveals the different aspects of Joy, while providing self-therapy for needed closure of recent emotional experiences. Fulfilling the expectations of those who were closest to me by writing and publishing is a big step in that direction. As a plus, the time spent in biblical review, and study provided solace and gave me a feeling of restoration and renewed strength.

In this book, you'll find my thoughts and interpretations, my discoveries and re-discoveries in the pursuit of wisdom. These writings start from my readings in Genesis, because beginnings are relevant. It's the beginnings which give comprehensive meaning to all else that follows.

My personal inquiries led to the books of wisdom: Proverbs, Song of Solomon, Ecclesiastes, and Job. Also, moved by Hezekiah's dilemma, I researched and compared his predicament to Job's. Both were men of God, who were attacked physically in similar manners. Both struggled with death from different aspects. The outcome of their situations proved very intuitive and worthy to share.

I have also included samples of short stories, poetic works, and verses to the youth. To add even more variety, a monologue of one of my favorite historical persons is included.

The opportunity to write is a comfort in itself, but to publish your words so they can be shared is a gift. I am grateful for the opportunity. I pray you receive helpful information and enjoyment in reading this book.

Dedication

For never wavering in your love and support, pushing and inspiring me to persevere. You are the reason I do what I do. You've left a lasting mark in and on my life, an eternal symbol of your unconditional love and sincere devotion. Your example of being such great parents, such good people, stirs my aspirations to be as you were.

Mom, you were my biggest fan! Dad, you were my biggest hero! You made me feel as if I can do anything and encouraged me to do everything. I miss you both *sooo* much. Finally, I am finishing the book I promised you I would, and I dedicate this work to you.

Thank you, God, for your divine foresight in giving me the mother and father you did, for I have encountered no greater earthly love!

Acknowledgments

What a gratifying feeling to have people in your life to whom sincere appreciation can be extended. Next to my parents, these persons were my greatest motivators. To my sisters: Vicki, Glenda, Robin, and Selena, you are what's needed when it counts. I'm still amazed at the devotion and love that has shown true, especially in the last few years.

I thank my children, Ebonee and Ivoiree, and my grandchildren, Amaria, Emoiree, Naomi, and Zariya, for their support. I love you all. Always remember, success is utilizing your divine gifts and answering the call God has placed on your lives. With God you can do all things, it's in you! Here's to you and to your many accomplishments throughout your lifetimes. Keep the focus, God first!

Thank you Pastors Camp and family for all your loving support with the family and ministry. My committed prayer partners—Sisters' Marion, Ann; Pastors Harriet and Hannah; Chief Banks and Brother Dave, I appreciate your help and prayers through the years! Thank you to all my nieces and nephews, particularly, Karen, Arnecia, and Victoria for your commitment to the ministry. Thank you, Steve, for the magnificent illustrations! You guys are the best!

Also, to Pastor J. Washington, you guided me to answers for many questions at a time when I blindly searched for truth. Your unique understanding and revelation illuminated God's word for me. You helped to define God's purpose for my life, and I will always be grateful to you. To the Full Gospel family, thanks for the beginnings. Brother Alvon, thank you for teaching me how to fast a lot, as well as pig out at Ponchos Buffet, a lot.

Much thanks to Cheryl, Vanessa, Ayeshia, Deborah, and my Australian Family, the Days, for friendship and support through the years. To the

KFGM members, supporters and affiliates, you will always have my gratitude and devotion. To Aunties Reatha Mae, Myrna, and families, and the One Accord Prayer Group Leaders: Sisters Ethel, Cousin Emma, and intercessors; thank you for your valued prayers.

You are all very special, and together we will continue to lift up the name of Jesus.

God bless you all!

May God continue to bless you and fill your life with more love, happiness, peace, and joy as you read through this book!

SOME OF GOD'S NAMES
ELOHIM – GOD
EL OLAM – EVERLASTING GOD
ADONAI – MASTER
JEHOVAH NISSI – LORD MY BANNER
JEHOVAH RAAH – LORD
MY SHEPHARD
JEHOVAH RAPHA – LORD THAT HEALS
JEHOVAH JIRAH – LORD
WILL PROVIDE
JEHOVAH SHALOAM – LORD MY PEACE

Before The Beginning

There was a time as I considered this wondrous world around me, I often pictured the Creator sitting on a massive, solid gold throne. I envisioned him with his immense hands under his enormous chin, considering the blueprint before him. I imagined him in deep contemplation over every detail of the pre-created universe and the yet-to-be created man.

I realize my mental depictions were inaccurate, but their implications were not. As confirmed through scriptures, God does put great thought into his handiworks. According to the word, God considers the end results before he begins creating.

> *Declaring the end from the beginning, And from ancient times things that are not yet done, Saying, "My counsel shall stand, And I will do all My pleasure."* (Isa. 46:10, KJV)

Through his word, we understand so much about the giver of life. We understand he considers a broader, more detailed picture. This makes him a purposeful Creator. Everything designed has a basis even before its existence.

> *The Lord of hosts hath sworn, saying, Surely as I have thought, so shall it come to pass; and as I have purposed, so shall it stand.* (Isa. 14:24, KJV)

> *For thus saith the Lord that created the heavens; God himself that formed the earth and made it; he hath established it, he created it not in vain, he formed the earth and made it; he formed it to be inhabited: I am the Lord and there is none else.* (Isa. 45:18, KJV)

God put thought and consideration in his plan for creation. Yes, he actually does have a master plan, an unalterable blueprint, which defines his overall intentions for this world. It's revealed in his inspired word. God told Jeremiah, *"Before I formed you in the womb I knew you; Before you were born I sanctified you; I ordained you a prophet to the nations"* (Jer. 1:5, KJV).

You can discover much of God's original plans for man in the book of Genesis and the Garden of Eden. Man was created to live and fellowship with God forever. He was to live a sin-free, worry-free, sickness-free, and disease-free existence. He was given authority in a territory where he was to dominate all other creations (Gen.1:26, KJV). That purpose is still in effect and will be completely manifested one day (Isa. 14:24**).

How did our Creator come into existence? That is an excellent question. As with all matters requiring such answers, we should consult the word of God. It reveals to us these facts: before there were the heavens, before there was the earth, God existed. Before there was space, matter, or time, God existed. Ultimately, there was no pre-creation, only the everlasting (eternal, ceaseless) God. He was here before the beginning; nothing caused his existence. In Isaiah 43:10–11, KJV God speaks:

> *Ye are my witnesses, saith the Lord, and my servant*
> *whom I have chosen: that ye may know and believe*
> *me, and understand that I am he: before me there was*
> *no God formed, neither shall there be after me. I, even*
> *I, am the Lord; and beside me there is no saviour.*

Time, matter, and space, did not exist until God spoke the universe into reality. When God said "Let there be" (Gen. 1), then and only then, there was. There was no worldly reality of the tangible or intangible before God spoke it. Therefore, there was no "before time" to consider. There was only the eternal God who is self-existent. He is independent of any entity or sources. He was never created; he did not evolve from an explosion in the universe. In fact, there is no sound scientific explanation or theory that can naturally explain God's existence. God is supernatural and can only be explained by supernatural means. God has always been, and forever shall be (Gen. 1:1**).

Man Is Significant To God

Through the book of Genesis, we can see the creative power in God's words. God said and God saw. Yet when God made man, he took the time to form, to shape mankind with his very hands (Gen. 1:26, 2:7**). He molded man into his image and made certain the image resembled its Creator. God breathed his breath of life into the nostrils of man, giving him life. God imparted his pure nature within man.

Though God also formed animals from dust, he gave man authority to name them. To further assert man's significance, God entrusted him with the authority over earth's dominion. All that God created was to accommodate the being that he so loved. Man was created for God's pleasure, to enjoy his fellowship and his glory.

> *Thou art worthy, O Lord, to receive glory and honour and power: for thou hast created all things, and for thy pleasure they are and were created.* (Rev. 4:11, KJV)

God did not create man or the universe out of necessity. He needs nothing or anyone. God is self-sufficient and every part of this world was brought into existence on his own accord. God could have spoken man into existence. This was his method for all else except man and animals. Even though both were created from dirt, only man was created in the image of God. His angels dwell with him, but they were not created in his image. God's considerations for humankind shows their importance above all else.

King David marveled at the complexities and sophistication of God's cosmological designs. God's details to the order in which he established the solar system fascinated David. In comparison to the vastness of the heavens, there is mere man made from the dust of the earth. Yet, he holds a superlative place of authority over all God's creations.

David expressed his observation and amazement so eloquently in Psalms 8:3–6, KVJ.

> *When I consider thy heavens, the work of thy fingers, the moon and the stars, which thou hast ordained; What is man, that thou art mindful of him? and the son of man, that thou visitest him? For thou hast made him a little lower than the angels[1] and hast crowned him with glory and honour. Thou madest him to have dominion over the works of thy hands; thou hast put all things under his feet.*

---

1   Denotes the original Hebrew אֱלֹהִים 'ĕ-lō-hîm; which translates to God (https://biblehub.com/text/psalms/8-5.htm)

THE GARDEN OF EDEN

The Garden Of Eden

God planted a garden east of Eden, a flawless work of perfection. It was a paradise of beauty with ample provisions, including fresh water from the river (Gen. 2:8–10**). This is the place God fashioned for man to reside. Interestingly, God suspended rain to withhold growth of the landscape until man was in place to care for it (Gen. 2:5**). Now that man was in his designated habitat, he had the responsibility to work and care for his surroundings (Gen. 2:15**). Apparently, God intended for man to be productive and involved in his livelihood. Man had the task to maintain, improve upon, and expand within his territory.

God perused his completed works, all things he created were deemed good and very good (Gen. 1:31**). God was extremely pleased with his works. Just as with his other creations, He assessed Adam and his necessities. There was reason for God to conclude that this creation was good but it lacked completion. God decided man needed a suitable companion (Gen. 2:18**).

The animals had counterparts, ensuring that they would reproduce and replenish. Animals were great for company, as they were intended, but they did not have the expansive intelligence of the man who'd named them. They lacked the physical compatibility of humankind. Adam could not reproduce without a like mate. Man needed a mental and physical fit in order to have a suitable match. If he were to be fruitful and procreate, he needed humankind.

How fitting that the first book of the Bible is entitled Genesis. The beginnings are essential because they exemplify models for future processes and remedies. First, the heavens and earth are spoken into existence. The first creatures are formed and first man gets his first home. With his main necessities provided, he is assigned his first job, and so on. The first man also undergoes the first surgery, fortunately, with the first anesthesia. Verse 21 details the process of this surgery. Adam laid in a deep sleep, at which time God extracted a rib from him, completed the surgery and closed up the area. Verse 22 uncovers the reasons for the removal of that rib. With that rib, God skillfully and perfectly created man's equivalent, the first female.

God formed man's counterpart with specific differences to complete him. Most of all, man could now reproduce. Wo-man (mankind with a womb) was so pleasing to Adam, he was inspired and voiced these words about her, "bone of my bones and flesh of my flesh" (Gen. 2:23, KJV**). These are popular words we continue to hear at matrimonial celebrations today. These words indicate that wo-man's physical composition consisted of a rib from man. Now man has an appropriate help meet to assist him in *meeting* his God-ordained purposes (Gen. 2:18**).

God created man to rule. According to Genesis 1:26, *"And God said, Let us make man in our image, after our likeness: and let them have dominion over the fish of the sea, and over the fowl of the air, and over the cattle, and over all the earth, and over every creeping thing that creepeth upon the earth"*

God precluded himself from earth's territorial dominion when he declared *"let them"* (mankind). God gave the authority to rule earth's dominion over to man.

Initially, dominion over the earth was decreed to Adam and Eve collectively. God commanded them to fill the earth and subdue it, to rule over all his earthly creations (Gen. 1:28**). By this means, God is sharing his authority with man for earth's realm. Man has been given rulership, not ownership. As creator of the world, God own's the earth and the fullness thereof (Ps. 24:1, 1 Cor. 10:26**). That fact will never change.

Sin Enters

In summary, after God created the Garden of Eden, he made Adam to dwell within and care for it. God then created Eve, his suitable counterpart to help him. Male and female were created sinless, in a sin-free environment. Though the environment was sin-free, apparently, it was not Satan free.

God provided man with everything needed to follow his commands of dominion, productivity, and expansion. He gave man another instruction in Genesis 2:17, KJV:

> *But of the tree of the knowledge of good and evil, thou shalt not eat of it: for in the day that thou eatest thereof thou shalt surely die.*

It seems that Satan was also lurking about in the garden. It appears he was going to and fro gathering intel, waiting for the proper time to strike. He'd somehow attained the knowledge needed to create a deadly plan of deception. Satan successfully strategized to open the door to sin. Still today he continues in his methods of operation, going to and fro gathering deadly intel against mankind. This is why we are admonished to remain vigilant. Our greatest foe, Satan, waits for the opportune moment to strike a deadly blow (1 Pet. 5:8**).

In the third chapter of Genesis, we learn of the serpent and its characteristics. According to verse 1, of all the animals God created, the serpent was the most subtil. The definition of this word, according to the online King James Version (KJV) Dictionary: Sly; artful; cunning; crafty; insinuating; as a subtil person; a subtil adversary (KJV Dictionary Definition: subtil). It is essential to note that God did not give the snake these traits to commit evil. Remember God pronounced his creations good and very good. There was no evil in God's nature; therefore, he could not have breathed evil into the nostrils of his creations. These were good qualities that were used in an evil way.

This snake was just that "a snake." It was persuaded to be a participant with Satan in the fall of man. The Bible says the snake was a *beast* of the field (Gen. 3:1**). It obviously possessed human qualities. Whether the ability to talk was a part of its original makeup or came about as a result of being possessed by Satan, is unclear. But the snake did verbally communicate. It had a form of intellect, and prior to the role in man's fall, it walked upright. Based upon Eve's reaction, it must have been a common occurrence to see and converse with the snake in Eden. According to scripture, there was no signs of Eve being surprised or startled by the snake or his talking abilities. This has so many implications. Nevertheless, Satan was involved, for he was also cursed. The snake's craftiness and apparent frequency in the garden made it a leading candidate to Satan's deceptive plan.

The plan was in effect, and the woman was the agreed-upon target. The strategy was obviously to subtly sow lies to cause the woman to doubt God. The ploy continued, triggering the woman to question God's love and integrity. Isn't that the same today? When we lose our spiritual focus, the enemy is right there to take advantage of the opportunity to deceive. There are many forms and circumstances our adversary uses. Most times the people and situations dearest or closest to us are spiritually manipulated. It is a spiritual battle we engage in, not flesh and blood. One that is influenced by Satan and his demonic forces (Eph. 6:12**). No matter his form or strategy approach, Satan's main objective is to sow uncertainty and cause us to question God's love and integrity.

The serpent misled the woman with a twisting of God's words. Those same words Adam received from God and communicated to Eve. God told Adam in chapter 2 verse 17 that death was imminent if they ate from the forbidden tree. The serpent assured Eve this was not the case: "Ye surely will not die . . ." Here we have another first for humankind, the very first lie concerning man recorded in scripture. Lies perpetrated by the only capable source, the father of lies, Satan. Unfortunately, this was followed by man's first act of disobedience to God's direct command. For the woman did eat, and Adam, who was right there with her, ate also. We find here that God provided man with a free will to make his own choices, whether right or wrong.

Immediately, man's focus shifted to himself and off the creator. Adam and Eve became aware of their nakedness and tried to clothe themselves. Sin brought with it all manner of disrepute. Now in operation, sin unravels the "good and very good" threads of God's creations. Each culprit blames the other for their wrongdoing. God holds all involved accountable. The serpent was the first sentenced, losing its original status for its part. It lost its ability to walk upright, destined to crawl on the ground throughout eternity. Upon Satan, God pronounced a curse of enmity between him and the very one he targeted, the woman. The woman's offspring and Satan's offspring would remain enemy's forever. Woman's offspring would bruise or crush Satan's head, and Satan's seed would bruise the heel of woman's offspring. This means that Jesus, who was the seed of woman and God, would permanently afflict Satan. The devil's affliction on Jesus would be temporary. This gives us overwhelming proof that Satan was the mastermind. Even though he was cursed, he was the only one to gain from the rebellion of man. Our just God would never have pronounced a curse on Satan had he not been involved.

The woman was now cursed with pain and sorrow during childbirth. She lost her equality with her husband who would now rule over her. Adam would no longer have an easy time of working the grounds which were also cursed. The grounds would now yield thistles, thorns and the likes, contributing to man's sweat inducing toil. He was condemned to hard work for sustenance to survive. The consequences of man's disobedience turned the perfectly created world into a fallen one. All the animals and mankind would now die physically and return to the source from which they were created.

The first eviction takes place, dislodging Adam and Eve from their home in Eden. To block their return; God placed a cherubim and a rotating sword to prevent their re-entrance into the garden. Man, who was given the authority to dominate now resides under Satan's domain as the one dominated.

SIDEBAR: When we try and define sin, we must realize that it is not just our actions that go against the word of God. We should look at the root of those actions. We have to recognize the fact that due to the actions of the first man, Adam, all men have a corrupted or tarnished nature. It is that nature that is predominant and operating in man. That corrupted nature causes man to be a sinner before God. For he no longer has the pure, untainted nature of God. Consequently, man's unredeemed nature, in every way, is sinful before God.

Before the actions of Christ that brought about our reclamation, animals had to suffice as a blood sacrifice. These actions only served to cover sin. This is why we are so grateful to God foreseeing our future, considering our mistakes, miscalculations, misjudgments, and overall missing the mark. All things were taken into account by God when determining man's purpose. No matter what, God's purpose for his creation will never change.

The sin of every human being was taken on when Jesus died on the cross. If you look at it from a legal standpoint, justice was performed and the penalty for rebellious sin in the Garden of Eden was *paid in full*! Man's true purpose was reinstated, and his divine destiny continues. Jesus cleaned up what was messed up. By accepting Jesus and his eradicating actions conducted on our behalf, we can fully enjoy the benefits of the intended victory. That old life has passed away, and if you believe and accept what Jesus did, you can walk in new life (Rom. 6:3–7**).

It's Alive – Death is Activated

As with all else, God created death. Yet, death was created without life, it was dormant, inactive and totally powerless. As recounted from this book's segment entitled "Garden of Eden," man was instructed and warned concerning his boundaries. He was told by God that he could make a never-ending feast of every tree in the garden except one tree. These instructions came with a warning about the consequences if man disobeyed.

As we can recall, through Satan, the snake as co-conspirators in deception, and the rebellious actions of Adam and Eve, death was activated. Every aspect of death was put into action, spiritually, physically, and naturally. Mankind's actions ushered in sin and activated death.

> *For since by man came death, by man came also the resurrection of the dead. For as in Adam all die, even so in Christ shall all be made alive.* (1 Cor. 15:21–22, KJV)

Adam and Eve lost the sinless nature of God and took on the characteristics of the father of lies. They gained the nature to lie, manipulate, and lay the blame elsewhere. Adam and Eve took on the nature of Satan, wicked and immoral. The original fellowship between man and God died. The relationship of equality between husband and wife died. The effectiveness of prayer died. A life of eternal peace without sickness and disease died. The concept of eternal life on earth died. From the very moment of that rebellious act, the physical body began a natural course of demise, just as God had warned.

> *But of the tree of the knowledge of good and evil, thou shalt not eat of it: for in the day that eatest thereof thou shalt surely die.* (Gen. 2:17, KJV)

Eventually, as with Adam and Eve, their descendants and all creatures are sentenced to die a physical death.

SOME OF SATAN'S NAMES
LUCIFER - MORNING STAR
(BEFORE HIS REBELLION)
SATAN - ADVERSARY, ACCUSER
DEVIL - TO SEPARATE
DEMON - EVIL SPIRIT
TEMPTER - TO PROVOKE, ENTICE
BEELZEBUL - CHIEF DEVIL
LIAR, THIEF, MURDER
OLD SERPENT
DECEIVER OF THE WORLD

Who Is Satan?

We briefly examined the beginnings. We moved forward to discover how man gained and lost dominion and authority. We should briefly explore the being that deprived man of his divine empowerment. Although we first read about Satan in the book of Genesis, more details are found in the book of Isaiah. Information providing details on God's good creation who became evil.

> How art thou fallen from heaven, O Lucifer, son of morning! how art thou cut down to the ground, which didst weaken the nations! For thou hast said in thine heart, I will ascend into heaven, I will exalt my throne above the stars of God: I will sit also upon the mount of the congregation, in the sides of the north: I will ascend above the heights of the clouds; I will be like the most High. (Isa. 14:12–14, KJV)

First, we should understand the fact that Satan is not a god, and is not equal to the one true God. The true God possesses infinite power, and wields omni characteristics. Traits which separate the Creator from those things created. None of God's supreme abilities or qualities are possessed by Satan. Satan himself was created by God. The Bible tells us that God created all things (entirety, everything) (Gen. 1:31**). There is no place or creature in heaven or on earth that God did not create.

We conclude several facts from the passage in Isaiah. There was an angel known as Lucifer, son of the morning, who attempted to elevate himself above God's creations. He was an angel, and God had already gifted him as a high and exalted creature. According to scripture, he dwelled in heaven with God at one time. Consequently, his desire was to become equal with God.

Lucifer was not created with sin or wickedness in his nature. Again, because of God's sinless, loving nature, all of God's creations were created without sin. We can get a keen insight of the origins of jealousy, pride, and greed when studying this part of scripture. We find Lucifer had illusions of utmost grandeur. In the book of Ezekiel 28:12–15**, we read more of the story concerning Lucifer's position and fall. This particular text begins with the prophet Ezekiel pronouncing prophetic laments upon the City of Tyre and its Prince. As we continue to read, we find that the prophet begins to highlight the supernatural force behind the egotistical, sinful actions of the king. Just as it was with the snake in the Garden of Eden, the true culprit, the puppeteer, Satan, is called out.

According to these scriptural accounts, Lucifer was an angel. He was perfect in beauty and wisdom. He was *the* anointed cherub, one of a kind. He was beautified in precious stones, and his vocal cords were musical instruments. This indicates that Lucifer was gifted with great musical abilities. We also find that he had a covering wing span and was a protector of God's throne. God allowed him access to his holy mountain and liberty to travel where God himself traveled. He even had **access to Eden**, God's garden.

Lucifer was honored by God, who adorned him in beauty, privilege, and power. Beginning in verse 12, we discover the internal and external grandeur bestowed on Lucifer twisted his perception of who and why he was created. He became wicked. When I see this word, wicked, I often think of wicker. Both words come from the same root of the old Anglo-Saxon word wiker or "wicker" which means to twist, (Blank 2017). For example, wicker furniture, the cane-like furniture known for being twisted and entwined. The good within and the truth becomes twisted with negative, self-perceptions. Eventually, the good becomes contaminated. If allowed to continue, unchecked, the end result is evilness or wickedness.

There are many speculations from different analyses concerning Lucifer's spiritual breakdown. Verse 15 says that "iniquity was found within him." Lucifer had more than any being could ask for, yet he wanted more. He ultimately wanted to be God. Somewhere in his twisted mind he thought he could be God. We can see and understand God gave man, as well as angels, free will to make their own choices. It shows the integrity of God, for he **permits** the choices we make.

This indeed was not a good choice by Lucifer, for there was no way he could succeed. Even though he was a very powerful being (bestowed by God), God is all-powerful. Lucifer lacked the qualities and abilities to be God. He was not and could not become God! He had none of the omni capabilities, and he could not create. He allowed himself to become vain and pridefully engrossed in the creature, and became disconnected from the essence of the Creator. He became delusional and acted on his erroneous notions.

Yet, Lucifer was extremely persuasive. I expect this was due to the leadership calling God bestowed upon him. Lucifer convinced one-third of the angels in heaven to join him in a hostile takeover. Lucifer led a great rebellion in heaven. The time is not specified. It was obviously before the creation of the universe, before Satan beguiled Adam and Eve. This resulted with Satan and his enticed army being kicked out of heaven (Eze. 28:17–18**). He and his followers lost their status in heaven. They lost the glory and honor given them by God. Lucifer's wickedness caused his nature to become corrupted. He is no longer that "morning star," Lucifer, but Satan. The Hebrew term *sâtan* (Hebrew: שָׂטָן) is a generic noun meaning "accuser" or "adversary" ... "to distract" "oppose" (Satan 2017).

Satan is the opposer of God and those who follow him. His nature is now corrupted, perverted, and wicked. He takes what God has created, allures and plots to steal and destroy those lives. His agenda has not changed from the beginning. He wants to be God. Anything connected with God is his adversarial target. He tries to achieve his destructive goals in their lives by any means available. His time is short and he will never sit on God's throne. Consequently, he strives to sit on the throne (become the evil lord) of God's creations. He will one day be cast into the lake of fire, permanently. He, the angels that followed him and all men who have permitted him to be their Lord (Matt. 25:41**).

SOME NAMES OF JESUS
SAVIOR – DELIVERER, REDEEMER
MESSIAH – PROMISED DELIVERER
REDEEMER - SAVIOR
ONLY BEGOTTEN SON
MASTER – TEACHER, INSTRUCTOR
ANOINTED ONE
TEACHER
KING OF KINGS
LORD OF LORDS
KING OF THE JEWS
PRINCE OF PEACE
WONDERFUL COUNSELOR
LILY OF THE VALLEY
LION OF JUDAH
BRIGHT AND MORNING STAR

Jesus Manifested

Even though we are all God's creations, we are not all God's children.

> Ye are of your father the devil, and the lusts of your father ye will do. He was a murderer from the beginning, and abode not in the truth, because there is no truth in him. When he speaketh a lie, he speaketh of his own: for he is a liar, and the father of it. (John 8:44, KJV)

Since mankind's original nature was tainted by sin, the only effective atonement had to be accomplished through a sin-free exchange. Jesus was the only qualified candidate to successfully accept our sins in exchange for his righteousness.

He was the perfect sacrifice. Jesus has God's holy nature and went through a human birth to legally reside on earth. Essentially, no being without an earthly body can inhabit earth legitimately. To execute God's plan of restoration, Jesus had to assume his place on earth as a man. The prophet Isaiah foretold of his unique birth.

> Therefore the Lord himself shall give you a sign; Behold, a virgin shall conceive, and bear a son, and shall call his name Immanuel. (Isa. 7:14, KJV)

Our all-knowing Father, in his foresight, prearranged this backup plan. God sent his only son into the world to reclaim God's creations.

> All we like sheep have gone astray; we have turned every one to his own way; and the Lord hath laid on him the iniquity of us all. (Isa. 53:6, KJV)

In Isaiah 9:6, the divinity and humanity of Jesus Christ is addressed: *"For unto us a child is born, unto us a son is given"* (KJV). A spirit being, encased in a dirt suit with a sinless nature. Born of a woman and given by God to restore our divine fellowship and relationships. To take back the authority and dominion from Satan, completely exonerating us.

As we can see, what transpired in the Garden of Eden is not the end of the story. Mankind no longer has to remain under the rulership of Satan.

> *He that committeth sin is of the devil; for the devil sinneth from the beginning. For this purpose the Son of God was manifested, that he might destroy the works of the devil.* (1 John 3:8, KJV)

Unfortunately, because of man's rebellion, we continue to live in a fallen world, where sin is prevalent.

> *Wherefore, as by one-man sin entered into the world, and death by sin; and so death passed upon all men, for that all have sinned. (Rom. 5:12 KJV)*

All changed after the fall of man to include man's original nature. Man, is born with a besmirched nature. This is why a spiritual rebirth is necessary.

Naturally, if we have breath in these dirt bodies, we must take up residence on earth. We must carry on our day-to-day activities in this fallen world. But, we do not have to partake of the God-opposing principles of this fallen world. We, as the reborn, no longer have to engage in actions that are nonconducive to a righteous relationship with God.

Love not the world, neither the things that are in the world. If any man love the world, the love of the Father is not in him. (1 John 2:15, KJV).

And be not conformed to this world: but be ye transformed by the renewing of your mind, that ye may prove what is that good, and acceptable, and perfect will of God. (Rom. 12:2 KJV)

We have been transformed, redeemed, and should aspire to be become Christlike-minded (Phil. 2:5**). Once we accept the given opportunity of the rebirth, we must no longer be involved in the world's illicit ways of operation.

What Jesus accomplished on the cross has provided mankind the opportunity to overcome sin and become reconciled with God. To literally undo what the devil craftily accomplished in the Garden of Eden.

We do not have to live in sin and suffer its consequences. The choice not to do so has been re-established. That choice came through the gift of Jesus Christ, our savior (rescuer, redeemer).

For God so loved the world, that he gave his only begotten Son, that whosoever believeth in him should not perish, but have everlasting life. (John 3:16, KJV)

For the wages of sin is death; but the gift of God is eternal life through Jesus Christ our Lord. (Rom. 6:23, KJV)

If we accept Jesus as the Lord of our life, we take on his nature. Jesus eradicates our past sins, no matter horrifying they might have been or we think them.

As far as the east is from the west, so far hath he removed our transgressions from us. (Ps. 103:12, KJV)

When Jesus becomes our Lord, we are where we were created to be, in fellowship with our Lord and savior.

God is faithful, by whom ye were called unto the fellowship of his Son Jesus Christ our Lord. (1 Cor. 1:9, KJV)

The process of replacing the devil with Jesus as our Lord starts with repentance.

If we confess our sins, he is faithful and just to forgive us our sins, and to cleanse us from all unrighteousness. (1 John 1:9, KJV)

That if thou shalt confess with thy mouth the Lord Jesus, and shalt believe in thine heart that God hath raised him from the dead, thou shalt be saved. (Rom. 10:9, KJV)

We must be accountable by acknowledging the fact that we are sinners. We then ask Jesus to forgive us of our sins and cleanse us of all unrighteousness. We believe and make a verbal confession that Jesus died on the cross, and was raised from the dead to deliver us from sin. A conscious decision to follow Jesus, to submit and commit our lives to his will is made.

It is not a complicated process, but a serious one. Now rejoice, if you have completed this process, you are a child of God. All heaven rejoices with you because you now belong to the family again, an heir of salvation. You have experienced the rebirth. Finding a good place of fellowship to assist you in your spiritual progression is the next step. Daily prayer, communication with God, and familiarizing yourself with the Bible. The Bible is your blueprint, created just for you, as a child of God. The only message for the sinner is repent, and be ye born again.

Pray and study your Bible, for they are material resources for effective spiritual growth and maturity.

> *Blessed is the man that walketh not in the counsel of the ungodly, nor standeth in the way of sinners, nor sitteth in the seat of the scornful. But his delight is in the law of the Lord; and in his law doth he meditate day and night. And he shall be like a tree planted by the rivers of water, that bringeth forth his fruit in his season; his leaf also shall not wither; and whatsoever he doeth shall prosper.* (Ps. 1:1–3, KJV)

> *Seek the Lord and his strength, seek his face continually.* (1 Chron. 16:11, KJV)

> *Then shall ye call upon me, and ye shall go and pray unto me, and I will hearken unto you.* (Jer. 29:12, KJV)

> *Confess your faults one to another, and pray one for another, that ye may be healed. The effectual fervent prayer of a righteous man availeth much.* (James 5:16, KJV)

> *If my people, which are called by my name, shall humble themselves, and pray, and seek my face, and turn from their wicked ways; then will I hear from heaven, and will forgive their sin, and will heal their land.* (2 Chron. 7:14, KJV)

These are just a few important scriptures concerning ways to seek, obtain knowledge and secure the strength of God through prayer and biblical revelation. There are so many more golden nuggets in the Bible. All is available to help us gain and maintain the victory in our new walk with God. As we read the Bible, we discover that manifested prayer consists of praying God's word. As his children, the God-given authority to pray with confidence belongs to us. Because, whatever we ask in his name we will receive it.

> *And whatsoever ye shall ask in my name, that will I do, that the Father may be glorified in the Son.* (John 14:13, KJV)

My Family, My Church

My family consisted of the traditional household—father, mother, and five of us girls. Five hardheads, as my dad would say. We received salvation, were nurtured and taught in a spirit-filled, signs-and-wonders-following, ministry. We were under the leadership of Dr. J. Washington in El Paso, Texas.

During an era when the Pentecostal/Holiness churches heavily dictated traditional isms, she stood against the norm. Pastor Washington took us thoroughly through the word. This was during a time when doctrines against women ministers, and definitely women pastors, was widespread. Pastor Washington stood victoriously against the majority. She was and still is a fighter!

Her ministry was filled with young people, one big happy family. She made learning enjoyable and left you always wanting more. She taught the word in spite of the opposition, bidding all to come. She provided the scriptural balance that showed the true concept of God's word disputing the traditional ideas that were incorrect.

As a teenager, I stood in awe of her biblical knowledge. She was a phenomenal vessel of God. The ministry was complete with manifestations of God's miracle working power. We'd witnessed blinded eyes opened, limbs growing out, sick healed, and the demon-bound set free. Most of all, we received the unadulterated word of God. Of course, she was not a popular preacher in El Paso during that time. She was a woman who preached harder and more accurately than many male preachers. Full Gospel rarely got invitations to fellowship with other churches. It was inconsequential, because we knew how blessed we were to have such a leader. Thank God for Pastor Washington and her obedience to the Holy Spirit. You are a great leader!

God blessed our family to start an outreach ministry that had been prophesized years before. In 2004, we started Kingdom Full Gospel Ministries (KFGM). The name signifies our Full Gospel roots and connection to the Kingdom teachings of Christ. We maintain our expectations for the miraculous moves of God. It continues and has elevated to even greater spiritual levels. The anointing remains ever present and operational. There is so much love, joy, and compassion within the body. Mother Durden, Pastor Durden, and Deacon Boyd were big reasons why it was and remains so.

It was in this ministry I first witnessed the dead being raised again. An elderly female visitor stopped breathing in the midst of Sunday morning service. Robin, the church nurse, noticed she suddenly slumped over. Upon examination, she had no pulse, her urine and feces passed from her body. Our small congregation began to pray and declare life over her body. Immediately, she began to breathe again. Thank God for his resurrecting power.

Near the end of 2014, it was discovered that Mother Durden had Stage 4, Non-Alcoholic Fatty Liver Disease (NAFLD). She'd never shown any major signs or issues concerning this illness. There were times when she complained of a stomach ache, but it was always in a "nothing to be concerned about" manner. We were shocked to discover the severity of her diagnosis. After the initial shock, we were full of faith that God would heal her. After all, she was a prayer warrior. She'd prayed for countless people who were healed and set free. It was a no-brainer. There was far too much work for her to do.

All were in denial, as we should have been. We did not accept what the enemy was trying to propagate. It was inconceivable that she would not be healed. She wasn't a drinker or smoker, didn't even use profane language. We were very ignorant about the disease, but soon became very educated. In concise terms, it was fat deposits built up in the liver. She'd been having associated issues for a while but the doctors were unable to identify the cause. It was eventually diagnosed in the final stages. Not long afterwards, she developed cirrhosis of the liver, a common development with this disease. Because of her age, she was not considered for a liver transplant.

Mother Durden was a mighty prayer warrior and a committed intercessor. Over thirty years ago, God directed her to begin a four o'clock prayer group. She was obedient to the call and diligent with the One Accord Prayer Group. She faithfully led that early morning group until her condition prevented her. Patiently, she taught a group to pray effective, fervent prayers, using the word of God. Today, under the ones she passed the torch to, they continue as powerful intercessors.

During her last days, she'd been rushed to the hospital several times. We made sure family members were there by her bedside. After her last hospital confinement on August 6, 2016, she was placed in my home upon release. This was a joint decision rendered by her children and a reluctant husband. Giving my father's failing health and his growing inability to care for my mom, he soon gave into reason. Since I was unemployed during that time, I was the best and very willing candidate. We felt that in the peaceful and prayerful environment of my home she'd be upward and onward again.

Mom was discharged one final time from the hospital. The doctors sent her home to die and were very open about that fact. In her diminished state it was hard to keep the level of faith possessed in the beginning. Nevertheless, the mustard seed measure was there and we continued believing. She could not eat or swallow, and was unable to take her pain meds. She laid there moaning in severe stomach pain. I sat by her bedside rubbing her stomach, asking God to take away the pain. I believed God would, I knew he could.

I kept imagining her sitting up in bed, laughing and telling old, funny stories about her childhood. I longed to hear her engaging in her witty, humorous banter with my dad. Even the exaggerated expressions she'd make when disappointed would have been happily received. We were in expectation mode; anything would have been a welcomed sign. She did none of those things. Still, we prayed, confessed life, and continued believing.

On the day of August 8, 2016, she was beset with pain. She barely spook because she was so weak from lack of food and water. I rubbed her stomach and prayed until she finally quieted. I laid my head on her bed and asked God to relieve her pain and suffering. Prior to her falling asleep, my oldest sister, Vicki phoned. Vicki immediately heard Mom's moaning in the background and began to cry. Through her tears she lifted her voice begging God to ease Mom's suffering.

What we considered as being faithful, at that time, seemed extremely selfish. As I laid my head on her bed again, I whispered, "let go Mom, go be with Jesus." I remember telling her we'd be okay and not to worry about Dad or our youngest sister, Selena. I assured her we would take care of them. Less than an hour later she made a peaceful transition to heaven after seventy-six earthly years. Somehow, though very weak but audibly, she called out my dad's name. Then she exhaled her last breath. I never shared that detail with my dad. He was already filled with the guilt of being physically incapable of caring for his wife. I am certain this detail would have filled him with unendurable remorse.

The following year, on October, 25, 2017, our dear uncle (Deacon) Boyd went to be with the Lord. A few months before, he was diagnosed with irreversible heart damage. They could not operate to prolong his life because of his age and lack of healthy veins. He was eighty-six years old, and fought for life. He loved life. He was disabled and during his last days fairly immobile. Nevertheless, we got him to Church every Sunday he felt able to go. During his last years of life, he received salvation and sought biblical knowledge with a vengeance.

He was Mom's older brother and was very close to his youngest sibling. My mom witnessed to him for years, encouraging him to give up his old life of drugs and crime. She prayed for him constantly. She encouraged him to embrace a life of salvation. A life that would provide a heavenly home when he died, and a victorious life here on earth. She sowed those seeds in his life for years, he finally gave over to Jesus. When my mom passed, he spoke of her often and how much he missed her. He was very grateful for her diligence in her prayers for him. He was proud of her being such a wonderful Christian example to him.

He loved to sit and discuss the word with me. At night he would let the word play over and over on his CD player. On Saturday mornings, I would go over fix him breakfast and we would watch good old Westerns on television. Afterwards, we'd discuss and expound more on the word. In the midst of all he'd gone through physically, he had become steadfast in his prayer life and his walk with God. Uncle loved God and was excited about and invested in his Christian journey.

Uncle fought a good fight, and told us he was tired. Prior to his death, he informed me that he was so impressed with my mom's homegoing service, he wanted the same. He trusted me to make sure that his affairs would be settled after his death as I'd done countless times while he was alive. Although I received immeasurable opposition from some of his children, to the extent possible, I made sure his wishes were fulfilled. I felt privileged to do so as his niece and pastor. I wasn't with him when he passed. However, I talked with him over the phone shortly before he died and promised I would see him the following day. Unfortunately, he passed shortly after our conversation.

In September of 2018, my father, Associate Pastor Durden, was diagnosed with cancer. On October 9, 2018, he went to his heavenly home with Jesus, the lover of his soul. I envision him ecstatic over being with his wife again, the love of his natural life. He desperately mourned my mom's passing and often talked of her with laughter and fond memories. He tried to continue here with us, but he wanted to be with Mom more than anything. I think he died soon after his diagnosis, because he was eager to be with her. He lost all interest in being here without his wife of fifty-eight, inseparable years.

He simply wanted to go home with Jesus and his wife. We encouraged him to fight, though we knew his heart was set otherwise. One day he refused to try another second. He would not take another pill; and refused to engage in spiritual warfare any longer. He could be such a stubborn and strong-willed man. Just as much as we were determined to see him healed, he was even more determined to be with Jesus. That was his constant conversation when Mom preceded him, going home with Jesus. His will defied every prayer, declaration, and every word of life that we spoke over his body. He was eighty-one years old and died with peaceful determination.

Three deaths of three beloved family members, too close, too much, too fast. The grieving process seemed to be ongoing with no end in sight. Each death would have us recalling the prior one. I was constantly blaming myself, entertaining the "should have, could have, why didn't I" game. I know the Bible and much of the wonderful things the inspired word of God teaches on healing, dying, and death. God uses me to pray for the sick and afflicted and God heals them. I'd experienced the deaths of loved ones before, but this seemed different. Maybe during the times we'd lost loved ones prior, I had not accepted the pastoral/leadership calling on my life. More than likely, none of the previous deaths were as close in so many ways.

The ministry suffered significant, irreplaceable losses within those three years—the associate pastor, head deacon, spiritual mother, and evangelist of the church. Major prayer warriors, adored parents and an uncle. These were some of the more committed persons, literally my natural and spiritual support group.

People you grow with, naturally and spiritually, complete a bond like none other. Working side by side with them in the pursuit and work of God, transcends the normal family ties. It was a sincere feeling of mutual love and trust, being covered and supported in every natural and supernatural way. It was an ideal team, particularly in ministry. Knowing that when we prayed, it was with one accord. Having an in-depth knowledge of a person's spirituality as they co-labor with you in ministry is the epitome of being in unity. The evidence was in the consistent manifestation of prayers, the church's spiritual growth, healing miracles, signs and wonders and the ever-present power of the anointing.

Even though I appeared to be at peace, standing strong in faith, my mind was plagued. I had the responsibility of being the natural comforter and counselor to the church and family members. It would be a great testimony to pen that I was unshaken or unbroken because of my walk with God. In truth, I was hanging by a thread, dangling emotionally, spiritually, and as a leader. I was even second-guessing the calling on my life. My mind was inundated with so many questions. My blessed assurance and shalom suffered major disruption. I felt like a failure.

Three of the most important people in my life and ministry died under my watch and prayer vigils. I wanted to quit. I did not want to be responsible for anyone, especially "church folk." I found myself going through the motions, literally pretending to be much stronger than I felt. Yes, I did feel hypocritical in every sense of the word. It was hard to come to terms with their passing away. I kept feeling there was more I could have done spiritually. I don't think that I doubted God or his word. Maybe it was my comprehension or lack thereof on healing and death that I questioned.

It was this state of mind that motivated me to search for answers, to conduct a more in-depth study. The following pages are simplified commentaries and insight from these studies. These inferences derive specifically from my study in the writings of Solomon and Job, known as the books of wisdom. They are understandable, and relatable. Who can't benefit from more wisdom? Also included is my study and review of Hezekiah. My interest was motivated by his relationship with God, his reactions to his struggles and their outcomes. It was quite informative and provided comparative insight.

As a Christian, it should be my first inclination during times of unrest or struggle to seek the care and comfort of my creator through his word.

"He made me therefore he knows all about me." One of the famous quotes from the matriarchs of my family. I think it's the words to several songs as well. Anyway, it makes perfect sense when you think on it. He knows his creations inside and out.

God's investment in our lives is second to none. God has provided the means to ensure that his most costly or dearest treasure, remains whole and in optimal operation. He even knows precisely how many hairs are on our heads (Matt. 10:30**). How invested is that? He has provided every spiritual resource to assure his provisional promises to us. There is this magnificent masterplan manual (the Bible) for us to delve into and apply the principles for living our best lives. This time in the word, study and writing, reiterated - *God will never leave or forsake us* (Duet. 31:6**).

Every day we witness Satan's countless endeavors to oppose God and thwart his perfect plans for mankind. We must realize we are at war with the enemy because we are children of God. When issues and struggles arise in our lives, the best place to go is to our maker. God has not given up on his original purpose. Even when Satan deceived the creation God loves most, with sin, the thing God loathes, God provided opportunity for restoration. How can we not see how much God loves us and wants his best for us?

In the book of Jeremiah God says,

> *For I know the thoughts that I think toward you, saith*
> *the Lord, thoughts of peace, and not of evil, to give you an*
> *expected end. (Jer. 29:11, KJV)*
> *Then shall ye call upon me, and ye shall go and pray*
> *unto me, and I will hearken unto you. (Jer.29:12, KJV)*

Although some things we face may not be desirable, seemingly unbearable, and not fully understandable, we must trust God. He has a good plan for our lives with a preordained peaceful, good and virtuous ending.

BOOKS OF WISDOM

PROVERBS
ECCLESIESTES
JOB

Proverbs

I think it is appropriate to first define *wisdom* before we get into the books. I would be hard-pressed to explain wisdom without first defining knowledge. Simply clarified, knowledge has to be attained or gained. Knowledge is the accumulation and mental comprehension of information. Information collected through various data-enriched sources. It could be acquired through books, electronic resources, education, and/or experiences. Wisdom is essentially the ability to properly apply the knowledge gained.

During my lifetime, there has been several instances when I have heard the expression "he or she may be smart but that person has no common sense." As I embarked on a wisdom passage, I gleaned the fullness of that expression. Knowledge gained does not mean the impartation of wisdom is automatic. True wisdom manifests through natural life lessons or experiences, good sound judgment, and spiritual direction. Proverbs writes of King Solomon's explanations of wisdom. According to King Solomon, wisdom is essential to righteous living. From wisdom there emanates discernment, which provides critical perception through spiritual understanding and direction. It goes beyond the norm of natural guidance and comprehension. When there is insufficient basis for proper judgment, discernment fills that lack.

Wisdom is a teacher that is necessary for comprehension and just guidance. Of all the easy analogies of wisdom, an Irish rugby player, Brian O'Driscoll, said it best. Prior to a championship match against England in February 2009, O'Driscoll was asked his opinion on Martin Johnson, the manager for an opposing team, England. Johnson was also an ex-teammate of O'Driscoll. O'Driscoll stated, "Knowledge is knowing a tomato is a fruit; wisdom is not putting it in a fruit salad" (Cole 2009).

Solomon wrote three books in the Christian Bible. Proverbs, written in simplistic style, practical and full of wisdom. It reflects a more upbeat and confident Solomon. Solomon instructs the reader to use wisdom in their thought processes. Also, to treat and deal with people in a manner that is fair and correct. Solomon writes of enjoying life, relationships, and being happy.

In Proverbs 17:22, Solomon writes, "A merry heart doeth good like a medicine: but a broken spirit drieth the bones" (KJV) words to live victoriously by. Happiness is like medication with lots of positive physical benefits. Medical resources have referred to this fact recently. As with most scientific and medical discoveries, God already has it in his word. According to Paul E. McGee, PhD, laughter and a sense of humor are good for your emotional, physical, and spiritual health.

> Your sense of humor is one of the most powerful tools you have to make certain that your daily mood and emotional state support good health. (McGauran 2019).

There are so many great and simple accounts of wisdom from this book. They are very practical, sustaining guidelines. I found them to be helpfully supporting, specifically to help one in living a good life. What I found most helpful is the thought-provoking impartations released when reading Proverbs. The inspiration that causes the reader to take a look at his life, explore one's morality, and core values.

> *A man's heart plans his way, But the Lord directs his steps.* (Prov. 16:9, KJV)

In this short scripture, I received great encouragement. My sincere desire to please God allows him to guide and direct my course in life. How can my life's journey not be successful? God's wonderful wisdom is paramount. He foresees, predestines, and accomplishes his will as it pertains to man. Yet, even though God has established our destiny, it does not guarantee one will choose that path. He has given us the option to make a choice.

As the righteousness of God, he desires for us to take hold of his wisdom.

> *For the Lord giveth wisdom: out of his mouth cometh knowledge and understanding. He layeth up sound wisdom for the righteous: he is a buckler to them that walk uprightly.* (Prov. 2:6–7, KJV)

It is in his wisdom we find the power to make the right decisions, apply faith, and fulfill purpose. The book of Proverbs stresses the necessity of reviewing our decisions and positions in life. It presses us to conviction, and incites us to make applicable life revisions, renewals, or refocusing. If we want to be directed, we need to know the correct path we have been set upon and follow it.

Summarily, we cannot neglect our spiritual relationship through time spent with God. For growth, wisdom, and power, time spent with God is a mandated requirement. God has paved the path; though he doesn't make us walk it. It is up to us to do our spiritual due diligence to stay on the predestined path.

Ecclesiates

Naturally, I would be remiss in my discovery process if I did not review Solomon and his famous exploratory journey. The book of Ecclesiastes, never mentions the name of the author, but King David had only one son who was the King of Jerusalem, Solomon.

Solomon was searching for the meaning of life. He determined life was just filled with contradictions and questions that remain unanswered. He begins the book with the feeling that nothing in life makes sense. This is our heads-up concerning his pessimistic mood. It sets the tone on what to expect in Solomon's perceptions through his journey.

Solomon was considered a man of great wisdom. His wisdom was bestowed upon him by God because he desired to rule with perspicacity of mind. This, of course, was pleasing to God. Ultimately, Solomon acquired even greater wealth and was considered the wisest man in the world (1 King 3:9–12**). One of the greatest displays of his wisdom comes from scripture (1 Kings 3:15–28**), which details his mediation between two harlots and a switched baby.

Both women had recently given birth three days apart. In the night, the woman who had given birth most recently rolled over on and killed her baby. During the night this woman, realizing what she had done, switched her baby with the one born three days earlier. Both women persistently claimed they were the child's mother.

To resolve the matter, Solomon ordered his men to give him a sword so he could cut the baby in half. He would divide the baby among the women. Of course, the true mother's actions declared her sincere love for the baby. Rather than have the baby killed she would surrender it to the lying harlot. Whereas, the other woman, who switched the babies, encouraged the king to carry out his judgment and cut the baby in half.

By this ploy, Solomon discovered the truth and the baby was returned to his true mother. Everyone in Israel who had seen and heard of this occurrence was amazed at Solomon's wisdom. I think a decision such as this would impress the psychologist of our time. It was a productive mental stratagem that received correct and just results. He put his gift of wisdom to effective use.

In Song of Solomon or Song of Songs, Solomon is filled with life and love in what seems to be marital gratification. His happy state of mind is witnessed through his lyrical renditions and dialogues of poetic love. His main theme in this book does not pass on his typical wisdom as in Proverbs and Ecclesiastes. It is a beautiful song that celebrates love in many facets, God's love for his people, his children, and his love of the church.

According to 1 Kings: 4:32, Solomon created 3,000 Proverbs, and 1,005 songs.

And he spake three thousand proverbs: and his songs were a thousand and five.

The Song of Songs was just that, the greatest of the compilations. He had an obvious and passionate understanding of the intricacies of love, marriage, and sex. He knew they were a beautiful gift from God.

In the book of Ecclesiastes, a more downcast side of Solomon was exposed. Ecclesiastes gives clear revelations of a man struggling with the issues in life. Through his Ecclesiastical writings, those modern-day psychologists who might have been impressed by his wisdom would probably diagnose him with depression at this point. I surmised Solomon was in a backslidden state because of his lifestyle. He'd regressed on the teachings of David, his father, and turned his back on his first love, God. He became consumed with his fleshly appetites. These were the dominant reasons for his brokenness and spiritual disconnect. He decided life was not always fair, not understandable, and everything was just meaningless, vain and empty.

As a man of unsurpassed wisdom, seven hundred wives and three hundred concubines doesn't seem to fit his bestowed title. However, Solomon realized the women were not the answer. In fact, they were chief contributors to his spiritual and relational conflict with God.

> *And he had seven hundred wives, princesses, and three hundred concubines: and his wives turned away his heart.* (1 King 11:3, KJV)

He began to seek other gods and resources. This, of course, caused him to become heavily involved in idolatry. God distinctly told him not to get involved with foreign women, or women of pagan beliefs.

> *Of the nations concerning which the Lord said unto the children of Israel, Ye shall not go in to them, neither shall they come in unto you: for surely they will turn away your heart after their gods: Solomon clave unto these in love.* (1 King 11:2, KJV)

He disobeyed God. Ultimately, he rediscovered what he already knew. The conclusion to his search was to have faith in God. His greatest grasp of wisdom in the book of Ecclesiastes was to understand true wisdom is initiated with committed reverence for God. It is only when man is aligned with God he can truly find meaning in life.

I can commiserate with spiritual unrest, just as most can in the midst of one issue or another. Solomon made a choice, a decision to turn away from what initially provided him mental clarity, spiritual stability and great success. He fell into a pessimistic mental state and a diminishing spiritual relationship with God. He sought the external, ungodly sources for answer, which proved to be spiritually and naturally detrimental.

During his ecclesiastical writings, he was in a frame of mind that affected his outlook concerning his Godly beliefs and relationships. Rightly dividing the word of truth entails more than just discerning the relevant writings and intents of the Old Testament from the New Testament. It also involves discerning the authors' spiritual and mental status at the time of their writings. Solomon contradicts his instructions on life and happiness in this book as opposed to happier, more spiritually in tune times in Proverbs and Song of Songs. Even in Solomon's backslidden state, he spoke under the inspiration of God.

> *All scripture is given by inspiration of God, and is profitable for doctrine, for reproof, for correction, for instruction in righteousness.* (2 Tim. 3:16, KJV)

I realized certain revelations in Solomon's writings seemed contradictory. But this allowed a better understanding of 2 Tim. 3:16, KJV.** Ultimately, what is written *is* inspired by God. Even in contradictions, these words teach us how to proceed in the right direction and turn away from those things that oppose that direction. It encourages us to analyze the entire puzzle, not just the pieces. In the end, all pieces must fit in their proper places so the final picture makes sense. Everything must line up with what fits into God's character of integrity.

You know, I don't think I have ever attended a funeral or home-going service where I did not hear "To everything there is a season and a time to every purpose under heaven . . . a time to be born and a time to die . . ." (Eccles. 3:1–2, KJV). Either during the chapel service or graveside, you can expect to hear King Solomon's words in some connotation. Under the heavens, on this earth, God has predestined his purpose. God's purpose never changes. The fact that God has appointed a timing to his purposes for this earth and its inhabitants is spiritually reassuring. The good things, the not so good things, times of war, times of peace, birth and death, all have a season.

Job

When I read the book of Job, my mind is bombarded with so many whys. In all honesty, I become really uneasy, to the point of feeling a sense of guilt. It was hard for me to process the fact that Job was offered up, as if a wager. He suffered so much pain and suffering, the great loss of every one of his children, even financial ruin. I initially hoped this was one large parable. But no, according to the book of Ezekiel 14:14, 20**, Job is very real. He is mentioned along with Noah and Daniel, two very real men of God. Also, in James 5:11, KJV.

> *Behold, we count them happy which endure. Ye have heard of the patience of Job, and have seen the end of the Lord; that the Lord is very pitiful, and of tender mercy.*

Job is real, and his story is nonfiction.

Then there was the phrase "The Lord gave and the Lord has taken away . . ." Job 1:21 that demanded my research. I decided to really take a good look at Job. Basically, Job was considered a righteous man.

> *There was a man in the land of Uz, whose name was Job; and that man was perfect and upright, and one that feared God, and eschewed evil.* (Job 1:1, KJV)

According to scripture, there was no man more righteous during his time.

> *And the Lord said unto Satan, Hast thou considered my servant Job, that there is none like him in the earth, a perfect and an upright man, one that feareth God, and escheweth evil?* (Job 1:8, KJV)

Yet he was set upon a course of loss, sickness, and suffering.

It is clear God did allow Job's testing in almost every area of his life. But unknown to Job, his assault was from Satan and limited by God. Can you imagine if it had been a full assault? He lost everything he had, except his wife, all this in the first chapter. Job lost his good health, becoming covered from head to toe with painful, nasty sores or boils. This left him in such agony he would use a broken piece of pottery to scrape his skin for some relief. It appeared he had to care for himself through his infirmity. He lost the support of his cynical friends and his wife.

Let me note that Job's wife suffered as well. Although spared the physical torment of sickness, she suffered great emotionally. She too suffered from the loss of children, loss of home, financial loss and loss of a true relationship with her husband. From her agony, she reprimanded Job into giving up the integrity he held for God. In fact, her solution was for him to curse God and die.

> *Then said his wife unto him, Dost thou still retain thine integrity? curse God, and die. But he said unto her, Thou speakest as one of the foolish women speaketh. What? shall we receive good at the hand of God, and shall we not receive evil? In all this did not Job sin with his lips.* (Job 2:9–10, KJV)

Job had been faithful to God prior to and through his calamities. He was dedicated and meticulous in his rituals of righteousness (burnt offerings for his children on their birthdays). Why should he give up near the end? Job appeared to be at the threshold of his heavenly reward. It made no sense for him to give up now. To curse God and die would have been to deny God, totally putting him in the destructive hands of Satan. His wife's solution was impious and foolish, but she did not seem to be in a pious state of mind.

According to Job at this time, God gives and takes away (Job 1:21, KJV**). This statement is somewhat confusing because it is contrary to God's character. God's character is that of a giver, and Satan's is that of the taker. This brings to mind a saying of one of my dear prayer partners: "God is about addition and multiplication, and Satan is about subtraction and division." I have always felt that was a very simple way to help determine who is at the helm supernaturally in matters. The Bible tells us *"the thief cometh not, but for to steal, and to kill, and to destroy: I am come that they might have life, and that they might have it more abundantly"* (John 10:10, KJV). How can I not add the most awesome-filled scripture that shows the nature of a giver?

> *For God so loved the world that he gave his only begotten son, that whosoever, believes in him will not perish but have everlasting life.* (John 3:16, KJV)

One has to take a look at Job's mental and physical state. It can accurately be concluded that Job's rash words stemmed from a grief-stricken, infirmed man. He had no answers to his dilemma or understanding as to why these things were upon him. He spoke, at times complained, from an anguished and bitter soul.

> *Therefore I will not refrain my mouth; I will speak in the anguish of my spirit; I will complain in the bitterness of my soul.* (Job 7:11, KJV)

This verse shows the raw honesty of Job and his desire to speak out from the emotions of his unexpected and unexplained situation. He was overwhelmed and unable to reason or to be "politically correct." Job was breaking.

Sometimes there are things in our life that need to be broken in order to be mended properly. Pride comes before destruction.

Pride goeth before destruction, and an haughty spirit before a fall. (Prov. 16:18, KJV)

It has to be dealt with for the sake of spiritual growth and effectiveness. Otherwise, you are not trusting God as the head of your life. You've taken that place. You have become the head of your life.

Most proud people don't understand they are prideful. How can they? They are too self-important and conceited. They consider themselves infallible. You have to acknowledge you have sin in order to deal with it. Sometimes it is hard for the proud to accept they have faults when *their* fruits show otherwise. But touch their fruits . . . well, we can understand by Job's ordeal how the proud can be humbled.

I found as I began to delve deeper into Job, it became more fascinating and revelatory. Overall, Job maintained his integrity unto God through his difficult testing. As you read further into his story, it is obvious Job harbored wrong ideas and laid erroneous charges against God.

It was revealed that Job thought God was unjust (Job 34:5–9, KJV**). He felt that disease, grief, pain, and loss were arrows being shot at him by God. Oh my, Job thought God was wicked. He even went so far as to say there was no reward in serving God. These misconceptions were neatly tucked away, and potentially spiritual threats. It is a strong possibility these dangers would not have exhibited themselves outside of this experience. Job was righteous, but as he finally rationalized, improprieties were hidden within.

The longer he stays in his tribulations, the less in tune with God Job appears. Job's self-righteousness manifested itself over and over again, as he declared just how good he was and undeserving of his trial. Job felt that God owed him an explanation for his tribulations and offered to go toe to toe with God to present his case. Job seems to be adding insult to injury for himself.

When Job took self-inventory, he realized his hostility toward God. His insight pertaining to God was inaccurate. Also, Job had exalted himself, he was prideful. Job became unfocused and self-righteous (Job 29**). In chapter 42:3, Job realized he spoke impulsively about a lot of things, stemming mainly from his lack of understanding.

> *Who is he that hideth counsel without knowledge?*
> *therefore have I uttered that I understood not; things*
> *too wonderful for me, which I knew not.*

Job concluded that he wasn't long for this world, that God had surely decided that his sickness was unto death. Yet he resolved to maintain his trust. He had to maintain/increase his trust in God. He declared he would trust God unto death.

> *Though he slay me, yet will I trust in him: but I*
> *will maintain mine own ways before him.* (Job
> 13:15, KJV)

Yes, he complained and grappled for answers. He never understood the process that put him on his path of misfortune.

Consequently, Job repented and became a better version of the man he was before his ordeal. God rewarded him for his faithfulness, giving him double restitution of all he'd lost. Of course, nothing can replace the loss of loved ones, but God again blessed him with seven boys and three girls.

> *And the Lord turned the captivity of Job, when he*
> *prayed for his friends: also the Lord gave Job twice as*
> *much as he had before.* (Job 42:10, KJV)

There is one last reveal for me I would like to submit to the reader. When God questioned Satan in his consideration of Job, Satan's response determined he had been walking throughout the earth. It was apparent Satan did his reconnaissance and had been considering Job. It was possible that he had other candidates in mind for his plan of destruction. It was obvious Satan was well aware of Job's natural securities and resources.

This does much to reiterate the fact that Satan is not like God. Satan does not possess the omni characteristics. He is not omnipresent, not omniscient, nor is he omnipotent. He is a fallen angel, not at all equal to God. Even less powerful than some of the angels. But he continues to travel to and fro, plotting his troublesome attacks on the children of God.

God, in his omniscience, knew that Satan was after Job, and if he could have, Satan would have killed Job and his wife also. Satan is limited by the one and only true God. Remember Satan's method of operation is to steal, kill, and destroy. God knew that Job was the right candidate, possibly more so than any other Satan might have been considering.

God out-strategized Satan, as always. God bragged on Job, highlighting him for this hard test. Moreover, God had a multi-fold plan. Through this, Job acquired powerful, insight about his spiritual walk, prompting him to humble himself and repent. Job became an even greater man of God, even more blessed after his affliction. God knows his children, and God knew Job would successfully prevail.

Hezekiah

The story of King Hezekiah unfolds in the book of 2 Kings 16:20–20:21, 2 Chronicles 28:27–32:33, and Isaiah 36:1–39:8. Hezekiah became king at twenty-five. His reign lasted for twenty-nine years. Hezekiah was faithful and obedient to the laws of God. He was compared to King David, who was the measuring stick for faithful, Godly kings.

Hezekiah set about restoring Godly order during his reign, undoing the critical mistakes his father, King Ahaz, made during his rule. Mistakes that caused the wrath of God to be upon Judah and Jerusalem. Needless, to say, Hezekiah's father was not a Godly king. Hezekiah destroyed idols that were numerous in the land, cleansed and consecrated the temple, made the priest sanctify themselves, and reestablished worship to Jehovah God. Hezekiah did many commendable acts during his rule that would be attributed to the fact, he was a man that believed in and trusted God.

In Isaiah 38, 2 Kings 20, God sent the prophet Isaiah to inform Hezekiah that he should get his "house in order" because his death was forthcoming. To be forewarned by God is the ultimate consideration. This attests to the close relationship he shared with God. God esteemed him enough to inform him that his time was at hand.

Hezekiah got the news, but he did not receive it. He turned his face toward the wall. After his death pronouncement, Hezekiah prayed. He put God in remembrance of his worth as his servant. He reminded God that he was a faithful, a devoted and righteous man. He did the things that pleased God from the onset of his rule. From the sincerity of his heart, he cried out to God. That was a nugget in and of itself. From the sincerity of his heart, he cried out.

It's obvious Hezekiah wanted more time; he wanted to live. From calculations in 2 Kings, Hezekiah was still a young man in his late thirties. Sure, he wanted to live longer. He was prosperous and had a good life. He was a God-fearing king; therefore, God prospered him (2 Kings 18:6–7**). Given the king that he was, he was more concerned about the future of the kingdom than fleshly pleasures. He wanted to continue serving God. The land was still in need of rebuilding and spiritual restoration. Hezekiah had a heart for the spiritual direction of his people. He felt that there was still much work for him to do.

This is a heartfelt prayer, one that moves the heart of God. He was not selfish in his request, as it would appear to some. His concerns lay in his serving God and his nation. God heard his cry and attended unto him immediately. It appears that Isaiah had barely left Hezekiah's presence, when God answered his plea. God extended his life and even gave him the remedy to apply for the pain and healing of his sores.

Hezekiah understood that unless God decided to intervene in his appointment with death, it would be a definite date. God extended his life for an additional fifteen years. Prior to his extended years, God also delivered Hezekiah's Kingdom from the hands of the Assyrians. The Assyrians were threatening a second invasion. They had already conquered Judah and were descending upon King Hezekiah and the City of Jerusalem. Because of the prayers of Hezekiah, God destroyed his enemies, and gave him a reprieve from his initial death decree.

Hezekiah made up his mind to live. In spite of the decree of death, he would not give up. Even though the order came from God himself, Hezekiah would not be deterred. His determination and unselfishness achieved the results Hezekiah desired. Still today God hears and grants our earnest, heartfelt prayers and petitions. God shows no partiality with man.

Then Peter opened his mouth, and said, Of a truth I perceive that God is no respecter of persons. (Acts 10: 34, KJV)

Be it king or beggar the same favor is available. God is not a respecter of persons, as we can see, but God is a respecter of faith. Just as prayer moved God to extend the life of Hezekiah, I believe he will do the same for us today. Setting our will with faith, being determined, and believing God will and does answer prayer - in hopeless situations these are sustaining essentials.

MY REVELATIONS

In viewing the situations King Solomon, Job, and King Hezekiah experienced, there were so many life lessons that presented themselves. The following are main relatable points from these brief summaries. Just reading and probing into the Word, as expected, blessed me tremendously. There were times, in the midst of study, I forgot my questions and allowed the word to wash and soothe me.

To restate, all scripture is inspired by God. Through this verse I started my check list. It teaches (check), rebukes (check, check), corrects (check, check, check), and trains us to align with God (check, infinity). I completed this time of study mainly realizing I needed more trust in Jesus. I saw a fragment of myself in each of the persons I studied. Naturally, I found myself repenting and weeping.

It is in the time of hardships that we can discover what is really inside. I don't think it's a bad thing to wonder or ask why. Jesus asked why on the cross.

> *And about the ninth hour Jesus cried with a loud voice, saying, Eli, Eli, lama sabachthani? that is to say, My God, my God, why hast thou forsaken me?* (Matt. 27:46, KJV)

The danger, as with Job, is when we interrogate God as if he has made a mistake, committed a crime. We get caught in serious pride when we think we know more than God, the omniscient one. We are children of God, but we possess no claims to his omni characteristics.

I noticed the differences in Hezekiah's petitioning of God as opposed to Job's. Hezekiah put God in remembrance of his worth, he did not do so demanding or as a braggart but in a dedicated, reverent manner. He did not voice his past actions of righteousness to justify his petition but to imply there was much more good for him to accomplish for God. God healed Hezekiah, extended his life and gave him the remedy to the soothing and healing of his boils. In addition, Hezekiah received more than he asked of God.

Job put God in remembrance of *Job's* righteousness and totally felt undeserving because of his righteousness. Job arrogantly demanded to be heard, because he felt God had taken away his rights. Job found fault in God. He criticized God. His approach to the throne was much more than the question why. Job threw down the gauntlet, so God took the challenge. Job, can you explain, watch over, or control God's creations? God questions Job. Job realizes his pride, repents and humbles himself. Elihu, the youngest of Job's friends, said in Job 33 (paraphrased): God allows certain remedies to expose sin, to prevent sin, not to punish. Elihu in his youth, proved even wiser than his elders, for he provided exactly the right answer.

Within the book of Job, questions arise as to human suffering. Surface-wise we conclude the piety of Job and want to know why afflictions would occur with such a man. Even though we never get the point-blank, head-on answer for this question, the realization is obvious. God's role in our hardships and testing is in no way punitive but corrective and restorative. God gets no pleasure or glory in his children's suffering and grief. His objective is life and that in abundance. If it were not for the limitations God maintains over the evil forces in our lives, they would be so much worse.

It's for certain God has reasoning in all that he allows. God's word is established and he abides by his word. He holds his word higher than his name, as indicated in Psalms 138:2 (KJV).

> *I will worship toward thy holy temple, and praise thy name for thy lovingkindness and for thy truth: for thou hast magnified thy word above all thy name.*

The established Word of God cannot be altered, and nowhere in his Word does it indicate that God is other than our creator, our Father, lover of our souls, and very mindful of mankind. God wishes us good and not evil.

Our God intricately created man. Even before our conception, he made in-depth plans for each individual. It makes no sense that he would execute such a wondrous plan for each of us only to toy with us destructively, or mercilessly destroy his creations. It is against his nature and counterproductive (John 10:10). There's only one that takes pleasure in our pain, loss and destruction, Satan.

These men of topic discovered through the many phases of their torments much that was hidden away in their hearts. How easy it is to neglect wrong attitudes when we feel like those things that are external are in order. It's those things of the heart, no matter how small, left unjudged and undealt with that can cause the major issues in our walk with God. These were all faithful men, at one time or another, and were favored by God. Each got lifted in pride, even Hezekiah as you continue to read about his life. Pride seems to be a magnet for the devil, for it definitely gets his attention and gives him a foothold. Remember, that was the main reason of Satan's fall, pride. That same seed of pride he sowed in the heart and mind of Adam and Eve in the Garden of Eden.

Solomon said that there is a season for various occurrences in life, as well as appointments man must keep. These schedules include times or seasons for war and peace, joy and sadness, laughter and tears. Ultimately, life and death, is fixed, or prearranged. Therefore, barring divine intervention, death will come to everyone at the appointed time.

My small journey has shown me plenty to work on in my life. Yes, there is the issue of pride and trust. I thank God for showing me areas that were put under the magnifier through his word. I do understand that God's ways are more complex than our finite minds can understand. With his creations, God is always at work, inside and out. There is a reason in all God does. We are in continual training because he wants us to be the best version of who he created us to be. Job's crisis showed what was within, good and bad. It also revealed that he was equipped to weather the storm. That was why he was chosen. God gives us the strength to bear whatever we have to endure. If we can't endure it, we will not be chosen for the test.

Solomon discovered what he already knew before disobeying God and seeking his own way. People should obey and reverence God, for it is God who will eventually judge all for their actions. He discovered that obedience in God shows wisdom, and wisdom is more precious than anything. At the end of the day, all will die whether they are righteous or not. How ironic that it took a backslidden journey to enlighten him on what God initially provided in instruction.

Certainly our path to completed purpose cannot be achieved without God in our lives. We see it over and over again through the lives we read about in the Bible. It is a given. God has created us to be victorious, champions, more than conquerors. We were built to overcome any struggle, weather the storms of life, no matter how difficult. Through our accepted salvation, we are greater than any and all foes. We are strong enough to resist and defeat the ancient evil and persuasiveness of our opposition, Satan (Rom. 8:35–39, 1 John 4:4).

We are heirs of salvation. In Greek salvation is termed *sōtēria* (pronounced so-tay-ree'-ah). Translated it means "deliverance, preservation, safety, salvation, future salvation, the sum of benefits and blessings which the Christians, redeemed from all earthly ills, will enjoy after the visible return of Christ from heaven in the consummated and eternal kingdom of God" (C.G.G. 1992-2019).

These things have been promised to us, that we may walk and live this life on earth in continual victory.

His word is an excellent source for the right kind of wisdom. It is important that we can study the lives of others, their reactions and outcomes. It's one of the best teaching tools for me. The Bible is my lifeline. It incites one to reflect and consider life and God's role in it. All the books of wisdom lead to the same deduction: the reverential fear of the Lord and trust in him is true wisdom. It can only be achieved through knowing him and committing your life to Him. We can't please God in this life without faith (Heb. 11:6**).

I can't say that I have full understanding of the things I have experienced lately. Honestly, I am not foolish enough to think that I ever will here on this earth. I know that there are certain things that we won't find out until we actually see our Lord face to face. Maybe he will make all clear then. Maybe we will be too thrilled to even care. I know my best course of action is to make sure my claim of salvation is sure, real. It is only in one's sincere acceptance as a true heir of soteria that puts one under God's coverage of unwaivering grace. True salvation is loyalty to God, and enduring to the end. When this earthly season is over, I want to be with my Lord and my loved ones, ultimately, the Kingdom of God.

I leave this study with much more peace prior to entering. There is an undeniable burden removing force in the word of God. Through this time, I have felt the power of God drawing me closer, revealing and setting me free from these death related oppressions. Literally, this whole process has been a remarkable positive, healing outlet from my brokenness.

It is for certain, as I reflect on all that is written and read, God did answer our prayers. For each received from God, a healing in its most ultimate form. They are today in the sin-free, disease-free, worry-free, death-free - secret place of the utmost high, eternally abiding under his almighty shadow (Ps. 91:1**).

I pray that my small journey blesses and enlightens you. Also, that it provides you enjoyment as you read portions or all of this book. Be encouraged and know that the more we search God's word, the more we are assured of his love and esteem for his creations.

SHALOAM

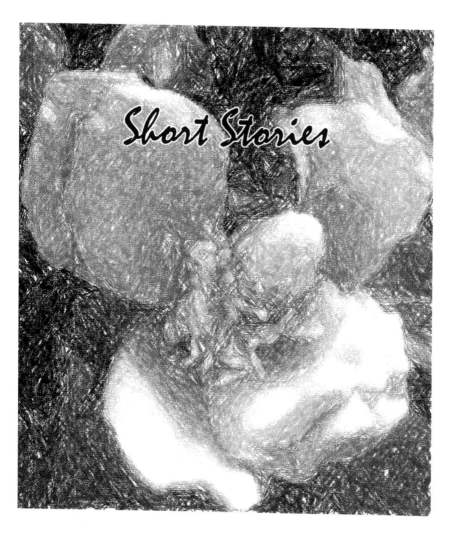

Short Stories

Well Done

August 8, 2016, is a very memorable date for me. Not only was it my younger sister Glenda's birthday, it was unfortunately the day my mother passed away. After the medical professionals arrived and finished their process; it was well after midnight. My mother's death was called on August 9, 2016. This saved my younger sister from the continuous emotional drain of reliving this sad ordeal on her birthdays. No matter which date it was called, it was still too soon. It all happened so fast. One day she was here healthy, joking, laughing. Then in one final, exhaling breath, she was gone.

The many things I recall about her keep me afloat; otherwise, I would give in to the sinking feelings of such a great loss. She was a great mother, but she took "no mess" from anybody. This included my six-foot-one-inch military-trained dad. She would allow you to present your argument, she'd even do the reasoning routine, but when it was time to give over, you were left with no doubt: "Give it up."

Mother Durden was very generous. It seemed she was always the one on the giving end. Most assuredly, it was mainly because she loved to be a blessing. It didn't matter if she knew you or not, if she could fill a need, she would do so. It seemed it gave her more pleasure to give than the ones who received.

I was the one who flew off the handle when I felt a situation was wrong or unfair. Thank God Mother Durden kept me grounded. She would say, "Just pray about it." Sometimes I just didn't want to hear that answer and I'd call my sweet Aunt Nae for an alternative point of view. She would say, "Don't worry, God's gonna fix it." You could tell these two were chips from the same old block, their mom, my Grandma Ellen. Eventually, when I would calm down, I'd pray about it and God would fix it.

I recall an incident in Rex, Georgia, when someone decided to decorate our driveway with racial slurs. This information caught the attention of a news crew from one of the local stations. I missed the live event, but I managed to see it on television. I remember my mom had the most brilliant smile when she spoke into the camera. She did not vent or show rage for such a horrible act. She told the crew that she loved everybody no matter the color. She further explained how she was blessed to experience and befriend people from all walks of life and cultures. She harbored no ill toward anyone, not even the artist who used the private driveway for his canvas of personal expressions.

As you can expect, it was a very short interview. Yet these words were proven every day that she lived, even when she died. Mother Durden was the name most friends and family called her. She had one of the most remarkable memorial services I have ever witnessed. People of various colors, backgrounds, and religions came together to honor her. There was the Holy Ghost singing, dancing, praising and worshipping. It was like one big, united celebration. As well it should have been. A true warrior had gone home.

What a driving force she was and continues to be in the lives of those who knew her. She was a strong woman of faith and moral convictions. She has always been a source of pride to me. As a child, I remember thinking how beautiful she was and wondering if she was some sort of superstar, like Diana Ross. She possessed the most beautiful smile and a laugh that was so infectious, it would elevate any environment.

In an era where there was a lot of black oppression, she always made sure my siblings and I knew that our destinies were not determined by man. The motivation and endeavor to continue in the midst of obstacles stemmed from her belief in God and family. Without a shadow of a doubt, Mother Durden was my biggest fan. It was no secret she enjoyed my biblical expository sessions, but after her death, countless people told me how proud she was of my pastoralship. That's when her pride in me really hit home. She would say, "You are as good as the megachurch preachers on television." I felt she had to say that because I was her daughter. From the conversations with her friends after her death, it seems she truly meant it.

I stepped out of my comfort zone to tackle and achieve many dreams. She gets most of the credit for it. This is why I sit here now to type this book . Her voice still rings within my spirit: "You can do it, you can do all things through Christ." That voice was a significant factor to my staying on life's course, when I wanted to detour so many times.

Instead of allowing me to throw a pity party after my divorce, she took control. She had to, I was emotionally drained. She would not allow me to wallow in self-pity, didn't even give me a moment to lick my wounds. My mom, with the solicited help of her sister, my sweet Aunt Nae, grabbed me up and took me shopping for career clothing. My mom bought me a new career wardrobe, even though I had no job prospects, no resume, and skills that were antiquated. At the time, I could not find a job where anyone was hiring a college dropout, unemployed mom, with passé computer skills. I know I searched the *Atlanta Journal* paper edition of the want ads. I did mention *antiquated*. Still with her aggressive encouragement, we marched on in faith.

That wardrobe was complete with what she called an "anointed interview suit." Honestly, that anointed interview suit has never let me down! Fortunately, after an interview in my suit, the federal government called me back after, let's just say, a lot of years! Today, both mom and aunt have passed on, but that interview suit still brings me much success. I know it is the favor of God, but that suit gives me that extra confidence boost. I am sure that the true love and compassion involved in its selection didn't hurt the process.

Around the middle of 2004, Mom encouraged me to follow my spiritual urgings and we started an outreach ministry. We had the same vision, almost down to the last detail. Our main objective dealt with reaching out to help young people in our surrounding communities. We extended our reach to the elderly, veterans, and struggling single-parent families. Today, we are still providing those services. Without her spiritual and physical help, I don't know if it would have successfully manifested.

Most recently, I decided to go back to school at fifty-six years of age to finish my degree. It was mainly through the influences of my mom. She was dying at the time and withheld the full disclosure of the extent of her illness. She scolded me when I wanted to skip class to sit with her. She wanted to make sure I'd not miss one day of class on her account. She convinced us all that she would be okay. I marched across that stage with my bachelor's and honors in 2016. She could not make it physically to the graduation, but she was definitely striding with me in spirit. She wasn't surprised, not even a little. She told me she knew I could and would do it. Thank God she lived to know I accomplished it. I can hear that voice loud and clear: "Now you need to go to law school and write that book like you've always wanted." "Sure, Mom, let me take a quick nap first," I'd jokingly respond, *in my head,* of course. A few months later, my mom was gone. How I would love to see that beautiful face as uplifting words flow from those prophetic lips again!

It was her belief and mine today that we should at the very least attempt to achieve every dream that lay in the deepest depths of our soul, every inner yearning. The Bible tells us in Psalms 37:4, KJV, "*Delight thyself also in the Lord: and he shall give thee the desires of thine heart.*" When he methodically created us, he placed those desires there. Desires that were meant to be fulfilled. It seemed that every completed milestone was our collective achievement. I pray that every missed opportunity of Mom's was fulfilled through all of her children's accomplishments.

She grew up poor and did not have the means to finish her educational desires. There was so much more she wanted to and did not achieve. Together we marched across that graduation stage. Mom, together we write this book. Together we pursue and achieve all we talked of doing. Well done, Mother Durden, well done!

My Chi

Chinese philosophy has a viewpoint that everything in the world is surrounded by a type of aura, a life-giving energy known as Chi. If you are whole and healthy, then that energy flows freely, allowing your emotions to be in sync and stable. But if you are ill—physically, mentally, or emotionally—then that energy becomes obstructed and throws off your emotional balance. I discovered inadvertently that traveling was my healthy energy flowing Chi. If my perfect little world had turned upside down, or inside out, getting on some mode of transportation to Anyplace, USA, made it all right again.

I was a Grady baby, born in Atlanta, Georgia, where I spent the first six years of my life. During this period, there is little to relate except paper dolls and awesome tea parties with Frunie, my best friend. Following in the footsteps of our mothers, who were best friends since childhood, Frunie and I had been inseparable for the past four years. Up until a phone call from my dad, I assumed a permanent continuation with the status quo.

My dad was a military man. Although he retired over twenty years ago, his Government Issue (GI) habits and old war stories betray him as being very much the soldier today. He had been away on military duty, either Vietnam or Korea, for almost two years. I can't remember which, but I do remember it was a place where he could not take his family, or as termed by the United States Armed Forces, "dependents." Now he would be returning, and we would join him at his newly assigned post.

Sheer elation followed that phone call. There was clapping, jumping up and down, and articulated jubilations of various expressions and, of course, ring around the roses. My dad was finally coming home; my family and I would be headed for new adventures. Still excited, Frunie and I started making plans at our tea party. This time we went all out.

Barbie and Cinderella were there, and if my mom had re-stuffed my Raggedy Ann doll, she would have been there too. Sometime later, my older sister, Vicki, who was about two years my senior, showed up. She had a look on her face like she was fresh from "Good Times, Party Busting Ville," making herself known with four shattering words: "Frunie won't be going." Apparently, it wasn't enough that our looks of shock and genuine disenchantment saturated the environment, so she forged ahead. "I asked my mom and she said, Vicki then spelled out, **N-O**, no!

Gathering my wits, determined not to be outdone by hearsay, I boldly retorted through forming tears, "Um hum, I'm asking my mama." Needless to say, that day became one of bittersweet memory for me. I discovered that only dependents, my dad's immediate family, enjoyed the privileges associated with this status. No matter how we tried to reason it out, my best friend was absolutely not a dependent. She would not be going. Soon we would be sharing our last childhood tea party.

Among the various dependent benefits were the opportunities for travel—oh, how I reveled in that benefit. Traveling, meeting people from all walks of life gave me a sense of anticipation and real excitement. It provided balance to leaving old friends by the mere reasoning of meeting new ones.

That sad day I left my best friend behind was ever etched in my memory. As the 1964 green Ford LTD transported my family and I down the highway to North Carolina, my feelings of forlornness began to dissipate as I observed the scenery. I remember thinking there were horses bigger than the ones John Wayne rode on in TV. All kinds of livestock grazing in wide-open fields of the greenest grasslands. Traveling was just the therapy I needed to bring me out of my solemn mood. Soon my sister and I were singing and playing games. I think it was I spy and tic-tac-toe. It didn't even matter that she somehow won every game. Life was right again.

Fort Bragg, an army base right outside of Fayetteville, North Carolina, was the place that claimed the next five years of my life. It is widely known for being the site of America's first public college, University of North Carolina at Chapel Hill. The Fort Bragg Army Base and the Pope Air Force Base are what gave this part of North Carolina its greatest recognition and remain the core of the region's economy today. We lived on this army base, which sheltered us from the big-city life.

Fayetteville, located just outside the base, was known for its uninhibited night life. The wild nocturnal festivities of Fayetteville seemed to magnify the uneventful environment of the fenced-in, secured base where my family and I resided. The "powers that be" created firm rules and ordinances that carried severe consequences for those that dared to disregard them. Since the punishment would be meted out to the GI for any rebellious acts of the dependent, my father made it unquestionably clear that should there be any untoward issues, there would be pain to the one that caused them.

Fort Bragg and Fayetteville, only a few miles between them, yet such contrasting environments made them seem worlds apart. My sister and I happily invited the pleasant, warm weather for which North Carolina is known. Mainly because our feet were our daily mode of transportation to school. We passed lots of tall green pine trees with tops so high they seemed to disappear into the heavens. I made lots of acquaintances and a new best friend while living there.

Lanelle turned out to be an even closer friend than Frunie. We considered ourselves sisters. Great times were had by all that were of our tiny, close-knit group. We could walk to all events anywhere on the base and feel safe. Saturday was movie day, followed by bowling and skating. Some weekends we would alternate with bike riding and other good, clean, fun activities.

Lanelle and I seemed to always be together; we even shared a true spiritual encounter, a religious rebirth that bonded us as spiritual sisters.

We both submitted our lives to God on the same day. As we both shared our experiences, it was clear it would always be the highlight of our young lives.

Growing up in North Carolina was a wonderful, fun-filled time, full of joy, laughter, and spiritual enlightenment. Unfortunately, around my twelfth year, my family, with two new female additions, was off again. I missed my friends, especially Lanelle. Nonetheless, a twelve-year-old had to do what a twelve-year-old had to do, especially when she had no money or resources of her own (Oh, and no rights). Goodbye, Tar Heel State, hello, hot, arid deserts of El Paso, Texas.

We remained in El Paso for about four years. This was the hardest place to leave. My first boy crush would be left behind physically, but I promised he would forever remain in my heart. Forever turned out to be until I got on the plane and saw one of my favorite movies on the huge screen. Off to the back woods of Fort Campbell, Kentucky, we flew. This was the shortest tour yet, residing there for just over a year.

My mom hated the place, and when Mama isn't happy, nobody is happy. My dad finagled his way out of Kentucky by accepting orders to Neubrücke, Germany, a small Kaserne adjacent to the Hoppstädten Village, about eight miles from Baumholder. It was there that the real world of travel opened up to me.

Between the school and family trips, we went on tours to Switzerland, Holland, Berlin, Austria, and did I say Switzerland (loved it)! Within the country of Germany, we went to Liechtenstein, the Black Forest, and to several musical concerts in Kaiserslautern or K Town, as it is called. Germany was so awe-inspiring my father extended his tour numerous times. When he could no longer extend, he was sent back to the desert. I guess it was a form of punishment for seemingly loving his own country less than Germany during that time.

El Paso, the place I once hated to leave, was now the place I blamed for robbing me of my magnificent adventures I had yet to fulfill. El Paso officially became the source of my unforgettable aggravation. That was until I met my future husband, Sergeant First Class Mr. Wonderful. Truly God is omniscient. He sent this fine specimen of a military man into my life to love and to marry—as a bonus, to continue my therapeutic travel practices.

How fortunate that he came along just when my father retired. I was no longer considered, by army dictates, a dependent. Fortuitous, methinks not, I have always felt that my spiritual rebirth gave me a great connection to divine favor and manifestations of my heartfelt desires. From El Paso, my husband and I went to Anchorage, Alaska. How extreme from the hot, arid desert of Fort Bliss, Texas, to the below-zero temperatures of Fort Richardson, Alaska. Much to my surprise, we actually fell in love with Alaska and extended our stay there several times. You will never guess where we ended up again—yes, El Paso, Texas, and finally back in Georgia.

With some reservations, I finally acclimated myself to being back in Georgia. Here is where so many major milestones took place in my life: the birth of my two daughters, Ebonee and Ivoiree, and my wonderful grandchildren; our outreach ministry; great employment opportunities; and a close connection with family again. Yes, and seeing my old pal again, Frunie.

Unfortunately, my husband and I experienced some irreconcilable difficulties and eventually divorced. Mysteriously, sometimes afterwards, he was declared missing. To date he has not been found. That's another story for another book. Through these major life events, I realized that the connection with my Georgia relatives and friends proved strong and unbreakable. It took my going full circle to be aware of that fact.

Also, I have been blessed with great employment opportunities. Some totally out of my comfort zone. It's beyond my understanding when

I think about this 5'4", 145 pounds, fifty-plus-year-old woman even considering some employment prospects so late in life.

Among the jobs that were far from my norm was as a primary officer on the Correctional Emergency Response Team (CERT) in corrections. Whenever I tell people about this part of my life, this dumbfounded expression is my first response. So I tell them, "It was like SWAT but only in a prison environment." That's what they seem to understand, and then they really shake their heads. It wasn't the position so much as it was the decision to go into this type of position so late in life. They think I fell from the crazy tree and hit every branch going down. Looking back, they may be right.

Well, except for the occasional vacations, my travel days seemed over. After all, I'm pushing dangerously close to the "over forty" mark now—okay, fifty. Travel, my self-declared emotional balancer, my Chi, was officially in the rearview mirror on my road to final destiny.

Then—*dun, dun, dun, dun*—out of the blue, a job offer via my old supervisor, Mr. Day. He was now in UAE, Dubai, and thought I would be a perfect fit for an opened position. He was aware of my travel therapy and knew I liked a sense of adventure. "Joy, Joy!" I heard my name being called once again! Tell me, how could I not answer my old friend Travel. Anyway, the period for much-needed, intense therapy had returned. It was just in time to take advantage of a new travel opportunity. Naturally, I had no choice but to bow and give in to the summons, you know, for the sake of my Chi. ***Namaste.***

POETRY
PROSE
CREATIVE WRITING

He Never Returned To Me

I've been on an earthly paradise since I met him two months ago. A whirlwind romance, understated;
Never has my life been so gloriously occupied, with nothing but laughter and loving moments.
Throughout each day, I would pinch myself, shut my eyes tightly and quickly open them again, just to make sure these moments were real.
Dancing, dining, cuddling, and discussions of the future; this must be love!
For my emptiness is filled, he has stoked my heart and soul as no human dared.
Love realized, without doubt, no reservations, assuredly, time has no relevance.

The dreadful day was upon me, he took his leave, he promised me only for a short while,
he left me with a lingering kiss, and reflections of the last two joyous months together, all I possessed of him until his return.

Days and nights of dreaming, then the appointed time arrived. Just as we agreed, I would wait at the table in the very corner where he first said hello, took my hands in his before taking a seat at my table. The same beverage we ordered, when first we met, set there on the table in the middle of our empty glasses. Directly in front of me, your chair would soon be filled with your gorgeous physique, then I will fill our glasses. How I count the moments . . .

I wave the waiter away once again with a smile that is not as bright and reassuring as it was two hours ago.
My heart is beating, pounding with anticipation—hopefulness. I began to worry of your welfare, I pray that all is well. I take my cellphone from my purse to call you, only to discover your number has been cancelled. How, we spoke only yesterday . . . ?

Again, the waiter returned with a look of pity in his eyes—for me! He spoke because his lips moved, but I never heard a word. My mind was swept away by our well-laid plans, your promises, our brief but unforgettable past. You said you would meet me here, and we would continue our wonderful times of love, laughter, and life together. You should have been here five hours ago, I have waited patiently, faithfully for you. No! I will not give up; I know you will be here!

Seven hours later, the lights are being dimmed as a silent announcement of the restaurant closing. Once again, the waiter approaches our table. "S'il vous plait," he says, "please, madam, I have prepared for you a most exquisite complimentary meal. To go. It is, of course, free of charge." Slowly I moved my head up and down in agreement. I stand to finally leave, determined to walk away with dignity. How I wish for wings so I could make a quick ascension, disappearing into the heavens. Yet here I am, alone and lost in my thoughts, in my blame; in my dejected shame. He vowed to me; on this day we would be reunited. This day we would continue our mutual love and adoration.

He never returned to me . . .

HEY, CAN I JUST WRITE?

Falling Away

Somber, inapt fervor, inspiration misplaced—
dying within, clueless to their dreadful fate,
Progressively, adversely, and surely regressing,
Forsaking a great salvation, discarding blessings.

Heart hardens, iniquity rises, Man turn around!
Lovers of righteousness, where can you be found?
No more crutches, the blaming game must end,
For it's you that's accountable for your own sins.

The cycle continues on with destructive behavior,
Pulling you further from the mercy of the savior,
I cry for you; you've turned off love, built up a wall,
Your pride lays bare, and it comes before your fall!

Gripped by carnality, blinded by fleshly appetites,
preferring the darkness to the marvelous light,
abandoning the giver of truth for the father of lies,
Don't be that person, who in hell, lifts their eyes!

We Roll!

In the thick of the congested traffic, we roll,
my brown, furry, friend, Foxy and me.
Soaking up some rays, with name-brand, tinted lenses
placed just so on the tip of my nose,
riding into the sunset, painting red the day, we roll.

Slowly opening the sunroof, allowing our hair to blow in the cool breeze
as we pass the Statue of Liberty, a replica, but a vision.
Foxy begins to bark at the pedestrian crossing our path,
she's dressed in her skintight getup, her wing tip stilettos,
and huge gray pearls, a replica, but a vision!

Strut on, girl, with your head bouncing from shoulder to shoulder,
I tag you Queen of Washington Street. Picking up the pace,
the traffic thins and we are closer to our destination,
that mighty Georgia Oak now in my rearview mirror.
Delicate sunflowers, arms upraised, basking in sunlight kisses,
now in front, as we roll.

Finally, we arrive, an hour spent on a twenty-minute destination, no worries,
what's been on my mind all day finally comes to fruition.
Lightly fried calamari with my favorite red sauce,
frosty Arnold Palmer with ice that seems to nestle an eluding lime
delaying inevitable consumption.

Shhhhhh, Cállate la boca, let me savor every bit.
Contented, I relax before hitting the streets of Atlanta again,
come, Foxy, settle in, **WE ROLL!**

MY FURRY FRIEND.

Next Wednesday

Each Wednesday, my emotional coordinated visits to your place of employment ensue. It is there reality clarifies the unwavering fear of being in your presence. Once again, mustering the courage to say hello is to be a doubtful event. It appears, the anguish of being rejected and wounded is much more powerful than this age-old desire. Therefore, achingly gazing at the object of my affection, will again be the prevailing agenda, this Wednesday.

My epitome of masculinity: tall, dark, muscular, oh so handsome, how you ignite my imagination! It is there we engage in the dearest of times, sharing conversations that reach way down in the realms of my soul. Then, at that perfect moment, right before our bond is secured with a kiss, you fade from my mythical obsession. Although, this repeated scenario is only make-believe, the pain is sincerely genuine. So dejection causes me to choose the security of longing from afar.

When you attend other women, laughing and flirting, possessiveness motivates me to make myself known to you. But then my stomach churns with an unfathomable uneasiness, my head begins to pound intensely, literally paralyzing all but my deepest thoughts. It would seem my mental longing for you has become a physical malady?

Finally, she walks away from you, and your eyes follow her as she departs, smiling thoughtfully. Still smiling, you turn and our eyes lock, this Wednesday, as if we were with one whimsical accord. Then you stride toward me with purpose and determination. Finally, today all things fantasized will become true.

As you swagger toward me, I become aware of the rapid rising and falling of my breath. I then realize that my chest is all that holds my fiercely beating heart inside. He speaks, "May I help you." Naturally I respond with absurd gawking and moving my lips.

Speak! Mouth open, words please come forth! Well, I am forced to appear as a gawking deer in the headlights! Still your beautiful brown eyes continue to meet mine.

Finally, my mouth begins to cooperate, the words are ushered forth as if jolted from a long nap. I speak, "Ah, no, sir, I am just looking," but in my mind, I'm praying that you can read between the lines. He is smiling and about to declare his adoration for me. Again, he speaks, "Take your time, ma'am. If you need help, my name is Gerard."

As he turns away, I watch his departure, smiling thoughtfully. "Thank you, thank you, Gerard, my love," I silently mouthed. Finally, love's evolution is in process for Gerard and me. Today the knowledge of your name has replaced your anonymity in my dreams. One step closer to true love. My heart takes flight as I anticipate what we will share

NEXT WEDNESDAY . . .

My Oak Tree

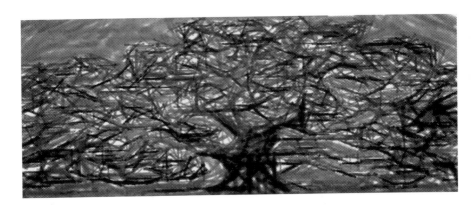

Outside he rests, antiquity's portrait of splendor, my oak tree.

His dark, thick, weather-worn timber bares his rustic etchings

giving an impression of two sockets, eyes that meet my searching stare.

Like fingers, his leafy lobes wave back and forth through gentle,

whistling winds, appearing to engage him in a seductive serenade.

Confidently draped in historical opulence, he endures nature's rustling and rousing

that lend bass beats to the established cadence.

His woodsy aroma is so distinct it obscures his environment,

accentuating an imposing presence, as if he stands alone.

In him, a silent essence extends far beyond mere perception.

Through every fallen acorn, every inch of sun-bleached, decaying bark

his longstanding stories unfold.

Tales that bespeak of yesteryears, simpler times; the blemished eras

that forever stain this land we now deem free.

So captivated, I struggle to turn from his world and reclaim my own.

As I take leave, musical harmonies amidst our surroundings release a

whispering resonance, bidding him to seemingly speak, nay, to sing,

"Go ahead, my lady, take your leave." "But know this, we are entangled,

as if a single soul; you shall never walk alone."

I am in awe of such magnificence, my oak tree.

Written Verse Messages
for the Young

Why?

What is the why of my existence? How am I perceived?
These questions constantly plague my mind, and I have yet to settle them.
Nonetheless, the truth of self-perception is somewhat realized,
for I am the future who has drawn its current source from the past.
I am a delicate flower, nurtured by the lifeblood of nature, but without love,
encouragement, and care – I would fade and wither till I'd exist no more.
I am a lump of unshaped clay, tossed upon the potter's wheel,
abandoned to the mercy of my creator, longing to be molded to perfection.
I am an undisturbed brook, quiet, still, yearning for that tiny pebble to be
cast across the waters, sending infinite ripples through the boundaries of life.
This path to my discovery is laden with self-imposed limitations and countless,
doubtful inquiries, but I breathe, move, and have being; therefore, I know that I have reason.
Even if my why is not fully understood, there is much untapped potentiality that must be transformed into certainty, as my search for why continues.

??????????????

Shy Girl

I wish that I could talk to you the way I see the other girls do,
I see your face when I close my eyes, I feel your touch as you pass me by,
I wish that you'd take the time to know my heart and understand my mind.
Take a peek into my dream world where you're my guy and I'm your girl.

Don't you see there's so much more, there's depth beyond my outer show.
Intelligence, sensitivity, lie within; a genuine heart of a faithful friend.
I'm a shy girl, but I want to be with you, someone tell me what I got to do!
I know this is not your burden to bear, the onus is mine cause you're not aware.

I just can't seem to get up the nerve, to get your attention and say the words,
I rehearse at home to at least say hi, I'm determined until you walk right by.
You roll through with your entourage, and look through me like I'm camouflaged.
Maybe, it's just not the right time, I should calm down, until things get aligned.

Right now I'll focus on more constructive things, I'm young and can continue to dream.
Eagerly I'll look forward to the day when I, will refuse to be held back because I'm shy.
This infatuation may then be gone, by then I may be singing another song.
But for now, if this is how it has to be, you're mine in my dreams, if not reality.

Street Life

The hood is not the only place where gangsters live,
Saggy pants tricked out riders, aren't alone popping pills.
Ghetto courts, uptown streets, there's a thin, fine line,
same sad faces, different places, it's just the dollar sign.

Education by the thug life, wanna be a street grad,
tough lessons are soon to come, ones you've never had.
If you think you'll rewrite the rules to this game – *Street Life*,
you may as well fight this gunfight, with your pocket knife.

Street life's a sadistic force, it consumes your very soul,
It twists minds and hardens hearts; you pay a vicious toll.
Slick wannabes, just like you, thought they could survive
the blood seeking, embattled streets and paid with their lives.

How can we sever these life claiming, street ties?
Liberate the precious souls, take back the mixed-up lives.
Help them understand it's bondage, not the freedom they seek,
What chance does the future hold, if we lose it to the streets?

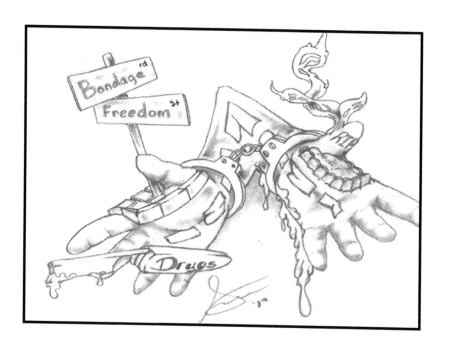

She Steps Lively

She is not a crimson-bikini-wearing, bubble gum, go-go boot–treading female,

yet she steps lively with all the swagger of a Bengal tiger sizing up her prey for the kill.

Not your typical, run-of-the mill pepperoni-pizza-eating, blackberry-lemonade-drinking sista,

for voilà, creating vegetarian delights that send the taste buds into a yearning frenzy, that's her forte.

Lover of earth, lover of life, natures beautiful, exotic flower, Bird of Paradise.

She steps lively!

Watch her with that stance, all the regal, poise, and structure of the Great Pyramids of Giza.

Observing her in her rituals of dance around the tall, Sweet Gum Tree, swaying to nature's offbeat yodeling echoes, causes the blood to stir and rush briskly

like the racing waters of the Tigress River.

She steps lively!

Oblivious, yet guarded against the naysayers, the confident thieves, the envious stares,

the crabs in the barrel waiting to get their claws in place to tear down her resolves.

Head in the air, back rigid like steel, eyes straight ahead, focused, walking the path to

Divine destiny.

She - steps - lively!

Death

I come without a notice, stranger in the night
you can't hide from me; I'll find you by your life.
So smoke your dope, crack and all
join the street gangs, I need you to fall.

Have all the premarital sex, your little hearts desire
cause sooner or later AIDS will put out the fires.
I come to rob you of your hopes and dreams
steal your destiny, that's the core of my schemes.

Try the drugs just once, that's gullible crap
that's all it takes to get you in death's trap.
I am here to monopolize your entire young life,
ravage your essence before you think twice,

Your age has no importance to me,
Be you one hundred, or merely three
Now go ahead, continue in your suicidal ways
I'm waiting on you to fill my empty graves!

DEATH
BY STEVE DURDEN

AFRICAN AMERICAN VERSE

BLACK HISTORY

Until I'm Free

Betrayed and abducted from my native land
beaten, and emasculated by the white man.
Shackled and stuffed on huge, overcrowded ships
forced into submission or face flesh, ripping whips.

Someone has to make them see,
I am not a man, until I'm free.

Forever separated from my beloved sister and brother,
how can I survive this, they stole my heart, my mother?
Vile heartless imprisoners, it should be you in my place,
experiencing such humiliation in this imposed disgrace.

Then maybe you could possibly see
I am not a man until I'm free.

Wailing in pain continuously, I moan to God somewhere,
My soul begs you for some escape, answer me, are you there?
Free me from this ship of death, amid this raging sea,
I'd rather surrender to my watery grave, and die with dignity.

For someone has to make them see,
Man is not a man until he is free!

BY STEVE DURDEN

The Conductor

(Harriet Tubman monologue, based on some of her actual words)

(The curtains open, in the middle of the stage are a set of railroad tracks leading off stage, out walks a woman with a cane in slave dress. She walks to the middle of the tracks and begins to tell her story)

I was born into slavery in 1829. I escaped to the North in 1840. I was free, finally free. Finally, I crossed the line to the land I been dreaming 'bout for so long, I was free.

But wasn't nobody to welcome me to the land called freedom, wasn't nobody there to take my hands and rejoice with me about being free. My body were here, but my mind was way over yonder, down in the ole salve cabin, with Ma and Pa and folks that I love.

(She pauses, slowly lowering her head as if to reflect, she raises her head again)

That's when I knowed; that when I knowed freedom was nothing if you didn't have a body to shares it with. That's when I made up in my mind, I had to go back to slave territory to free the peoples I loved. First, I help my sister and her two children get free; eventually, I help Ma, Pa and scores of slaves get free.

(She stands taller lifting her head higher with pride)

Folks calls me the Conductor, and they call this here freedom trail, the Underground Railroad. Lawd, I remember, I remember how dangerous it was and how I sometimes had to point my long rifle **(lifts her cane**

like a rifle) to scares those slaves onward when they went to whining and wanted to give up.

Humph, some folks say I is a woman of great strength and courage, I who growed up like a ignored weed, didn't have no notions 'bout freedom, being I never experienced afore. I jest knowed in my heart that a man won't a man lest he was free, and it was my purpose to do all I could to help him.

(Humbly drops head)

They call it courage, but I know it's the good Lawd and a whole lot of prayer. You see I prays; I prays all the time. I used to pray for Maser, I pray Lawd please touch Maser heart, please turn Maser around. Then I hear Maser making arrangements to send me and my Kin Folk way down South to works on the Chain Gang. So I Prays – Lawd, touch Maser Heart and turns him around, and if he don't change, Lawd – Then Kills him, kills him and move him out the way, so he won't do no more mischief.

(Shakes her head in memory) Lawd, I don travel this Underground Railroad, many a times and I ain't never came off the track. I know this here trail children; Lawd, I knows this here trail. I knows it so well I was a spy and a scout for the Union back during the Civil War. **[She lowers her head, shaking slowly back and forth.]** I know this here trail.

(Looks off into the crowd speaking loudly and with pride)

Then later on, after the Civil War, I was able to open a home for the aged and indigent Colored Folk.

(Lowers her voice and head slightly in thought once again)

Lawd, this trail hold many a tales. I know this here trail. One thing I always say is—freedom ain't nothing if you ain't got a body to shares it with.

They Don't Know Their Worth

Weary and worn from the cares they shoulder, no one seems to understand
the mental burdens, the physical weights and the emotional drainers.
The selfishness of those in their surroundings, takes them to a lower place,
they walk with their heads down, they speak but make no sounds, and by chance
if audibility presents itself; no one hears.

They don't know their worth . . .

Shadows drifting through life, destiny uncertain, purpose untouched,
though finite, visible, they remain infinitely unseen; low self-esteem.
Gifted, talented, intelligent to a fault, yet they cannot shake mental shackles
to break free from their oppressive, self-imposing cage, if by chance one dares
venturing out, fright yanks their yielding return to obscurity.

They don't know their worth . . .

I Still Remember

(Dedicated to Uncle James)

That little ole leaning church sitting across the way, I still remember it well, like it was yesterday.

It was badly worn, finally falling down, if you cut through the cotton patch, you'll see the steeple on the ground.

That little ole powerful preacher, Mr. Moe was his name, he'd gather the sinners in the church, trying to make a change.

He'd preach to ten souls, as if a thousand folk; he made sure others had, when he'd most times go broke.

I still remember that ole congregation, waving their hands in song, not a one of them is here today, even Mr. Moe has gone.

Those folks used to pray and shout so, and sing most joyfully, I remember how sweet and melodious, that sound was to me.

I remember that ole river that ran through the country side, they say it's the same river where the runaway slaves would hide.

They'd suffer the dangers of that river to lose the scent of hounds, instead of returning to bondage, many would just drown.

Although it's been near sixty years, it seems like yesterday, I still remember that little ole church, sitting across the way.

IN MEMORIAM

She Lives

(Dedicated to Mom)

There she lies, eyelids forever resting still upon her smooth, exquisitely aged skin;

she sleeps.

Without a word, she relates her story, an account that conveys life's countless journeys,
many tears, and much laughter;

she speaks.

Known for unselfishness, mercifully forgiving the myriad of wrongs, caringly embracing those the world has long rejected, traits that illuminate her peaceful countenance;

she loves.

Oh, how I marvel at your strength and courage, the lessons you've imparted just by being. As these natural eyes gaze upon inevitable physical frailties, these spiritual eyes behold a temple—that seemed immortal, possessing a beauty that far surpasses any defined by this world.

Yes, your spirit has departed this earthly place, but the soul of who you are, all that you stood for, continues in those you have touched so profoundly;

she lives!

Hero

(Dedicated to Dad)

The hero's cape he wore was not one that could be physically gazed upon,
He possessed no extraordinary tactical knowledge, no hi-tech ingenuity that could afford him the ability to invent armaments that would protect mankind.

I never saw him turn a vivid green when his anger went into mode overload to assail enemies.
Heard no tales of him scaling skyscrapers or leaping over buildings in a single bounce.
He couldn't catch bullets with his teeth, or with any part of his body for that matter, at least not without significant damage.

Yet his role in this world was to be a Hero, a shining star whose success in life was minimal by the world's standards but immeasurable by God's.
The needs of the world, if only afforded a small space, was designated for his special touch, for his special hero powers to lighten loads and inspire lives.

And his hero heart, that charitable heart could grow, oh so large, as he empathized with those who poured their concerns out to him.
With that hero spirit he would help them with more than words but with sacrificial deeds.
With all his hero might he'd help them knock down life's diabolical foes—**wham, bam,
kapow, crash!** – Victorious yet again!

Then protocol summons, he must return to his headquarters to recharge his hero powers.

Upstretched hands, humble spirit, bowed knees, and time in heartfelt prayer were the keys to his reviving power, so that he could continue on his mission of heroism.

He was not the traditional world's Hero, and he did not have to be.

Today

(Dedicated to Uncle)

Today, my time on earth has ceased to exist,
These mortal eyes closed to open in eternity's bliss.
Immortality now covers me, I can run and flail my hands,
With clarity I can speak now, with a jubilant heart I dance.

Today, I'm in a place where there's no loneliness, faultfinding or fears,
I'm continuously rejoicing, for there's no sickness, sadness, or tears.
For now, I fellowship in glory with my dear loved ones and friends,
Engaging in heavenly camaraderie, the kind that never ends.

Today, I saw my celestial mansion, prepared by Jesus Christ,
A promise he made possible through his ultimate sacrifice.
There is no splendor that compares to this majestic, glorious land,
Nothing can describe the feelings, when my savior held my hand.

Today, I am not sleeping, as many of you would suppose,
I am too busy walking streets, not paved but made of gold.
Fret not that this feeble, disabled temple, is at its earthly end.
Beloved, today I'm home with Jesus, my Creator, Lord and Friend.

Grandma

When I think of my grandma, there is always a sense of awe.
She would relate such tales of unbelievable things she saw.
She grew up with very little, you could say, abject poverty,
although materially she lacked much, faith was not a scarcity.

Her young life was not so privileged, yet you would never know,
her conversations were so upbeat, her countenance kindly aglow.
She was gifted with dreams and visions; they would *always* come to pass.
A veritable powerhouse in God, the likes of which unsurpassed.

There was a feeling of divinity, in the environment she would grace,
you felt safe from hurt or harm, you knew the Lord was in the place.
I have witnessed the power of God, flow through those healing hands,
I brought a blind acquaintance for prayer, true story; he saw again.

She would speak of things that were to come, that came; I deceive
you not,
if she told you a cockroach was going to pull a cart, hook it up and
watch.
When she passed on to be with God, I wiped the sweat from her face,
I used that anointed kerchief, and witnessed miracles all over the place.

Know that you are missed, Grandma, your teachings will continue on,
your descendants have inherited your gifts, some of them, pretty strong.
We are always aware of the God you lived for and taught us about.
We know him as our everything, a force we can't live without!

THANK YOU, GRANDMA!

REFERENCES

A Prayer for Salvation

Dear Heavenly Father,

I come before you, recognizing the fact that I am a sinner and I am in need of your help. I understand that if I repent, you will forgive and wash away every one of my sins. Forgive me for my sins and cleanse me of all unrighteousness. I truly believe that you did die on the cross and you were raised again, that my sins would be forgiven and my salvation guaranteed. Thank you, Father. I accept your wonderful gift of salvation and my place in eternity with you.

Amen.

ALL SCRIPTURES ARE TAKEN FROM KING JAMES VERSION (KJV) LISTED ALPHABETICALLY

1 Corinthians 10:26

26 For the earth is the Lord's, and the fulness thereof.

Deuteronomy 31:6

6 Be strong and of a good courage, fear not, nor be afraid of them: for the Lord thy God, he it is that doth go with thee; he will not fail thee, nor forsake thee.

Ephesians 6:12

12 For we wrestle not against flesh and blood, but against principalities, against powers, against the rulers of the darkness of this world, against spiritual wickedness in high places.

Ezekiel 14:14, 20

14 Though these three men, Noah, Daniel, and Job, were in it, they should deliver but their own souls by their righteousness, saith the Lord GOD.
20 Though Noah, Daniel, and Job were in it, as I live, saith the Lord GOD, they shall deliver neither son nor daughter; they shall but deliver their own souls by their righteousness.

Ezekiel 28:12–15

12 Son of man, take up a lamentation upon the king of Tyrus, and say unto him, Thus saith the Lord God; Thou sealest up the sum, full of wisdom, and perfect in beauty.
13 Thou hast been in Eden the garden of God; every precious stone was thy covering, the sardius, topaz, and the diamond, the beryl, the onyx, and the jasper, the sapphire, the emerald, and the carbuncle, and gold: the workmanship of thy tabrets and of thy pipes was prepared in thee in the day that thou wast created.

14 Thou art the anointed cherub that covereth; and I have set thee so: thou wast upon the holy mountain of God; thou hast walked up and down in the midst of the stones of fire.

15 Thou wast perfect in thy ways from the day that thou wast created, till iniquity was found in thee.

Ezekiel 28:17–18

17 Thine heart was lifted up because of thy beauty, thou hast corrupted thy wisdom by reason of thy brightness: I will cast thee to the ground, I will lay thee before kings, that they may behold thee.

18 Thou hast defiled thy sanctuaries by the multitude of thine iniquities, by the iniquity of thy traffick; therefore will I bring forth a fire from the midst of thee, it shall devour thee, and I will bring thee to ashes upon the earth in the sight of all them that behold thee.

Genesis 1:1

1 In the beginning God created the heaven and the earth.

Genesis 1:26

26 And God said, Let us make man in our image, after our likeness: and let them have dominion over the fish of the sea, and over the fowl of the air, and over the cattle, and over all the earth, and over every creeping thing that creepeth upon the earth.

Genesis 1:28

28 And God blessed them, and God said unto them, Be fruitful, and multiply, and replenish the earth, and subdue it: and have dominion over the fish of the sea, and over the fowl of the air, and over every living thing that moveth upon the earth.

Genesis 1:31

31 And God saw everything that he had made, and, behold, it was very good. And the evening and the morning were the sixth day.

Genesis 2:5

5 And every plant of the field before it was in the earth, and every herb of the field before it grew: for the Lord God had not caused it to rain upon the earth, and there was not a man to till the ground.

Genesis 2:7–10

7 And the Lord God formed man of the dust of the ground, and breathed into his nostrils the breath of life; and man became a living soul.

8 And the Lord God planted a garden eastward in Eden; and there he put the man whom he had formed.

9 And out of the ground made the Lord God to grow every tree that is pleasant to the sight, and good for food; the tree of life also in the midst of the garden, and the tree of knowledge of good and evil.

10 And a river went out of Eden to water the garden; and from thence it was parted, and became into four heads.

Genesis 2:15

15 And the Lord God took the man, and put him into the garden of Eden to dress it and to keep it.

Genesis 2:18

18 And the Lord God said, It is not good that the man should be alone; I will make him an help meet for him.

Genesis 2:23

23 And Adam said, This is now bone of my bones, and flesh of my flesh: she shall be called Woman, because she was taken out of Man.

Genesis 3:1

1 Now the serpent was more subtil than any beast of the field which the Lord God had made. And he said unto the woman, Yea, hath God said, Ye shall not eat of every tree of the garden?

Hebrews 11:6

6 But without faith it is impossible to please him: for he that cometh to God must believe that he is, and that he is a rewarder of them that diligently seek him.

Isaiah 14:24

24 The Lord of hosts hath sworn, saying, Surely as I have thought, so shall it come to pass; and as I have purposed, so shall it stand:

Job 1:21

21 And said, Naked came I out of my mother's womb, and naked shall I return thither: the Lord gave, and the Lord hath taken away; blessed be the name of the Lord.

Job 34: 5–9

5 For Job hath said, I am righteous: and God hath taken away my judgment.
6 Should I lie against my right? my wound is incurable without transgression.
7 What man is like Job, who drinketh up scorning like water?
8 Which goeth in company with the workers of iniquity, and walketh with wicked men.
9 For he hath said, It profiteth a man nothing that he should delight himself with God.

1 John 4:4 Ye are of God, little children, and have overcome them: because greater is he that is in you, than he that is in the world.

1 Kings 3:9–12

9 Give therefore thy servant an understanding heart to judge thy people, that I may discern between good and bad: for who is able to judge this thy so great a people?
10 And the speech pleased the LORD, that Solomon had asked this thing.

11 And God said unto him, Because thou hast asked this thing, and hast not asked for thyself long life; neither hast asked riches for thyself, nor hast asked the life of thine enemies; but hast asked for thyself understanding to discern judgment;

12 Behold, I have done according to thy words: lo, I have given thee a wise and an understanding heart; so that there was none like thee before thee, neither after thee shall any arise like unto thee

2 Kings 18:6–7

6 For he clave to the Lord, and departed not from following him, but kept his commandments, which the Lord commanded Moses.

7 And the Lord was with him; and he prospered whithersoever he went forth: and he rebelled against the king of Assyria, and served him not.

Luke 14:12–18

12 How art thou fallen from heaven, O Lucifer, son of the morning! how art thou cut down to the ground, which didst weaken the nations!

13 For thou hast said in thine heart, I will ascend into heaven, I will exalt my throne above the stars of God: I will sit also upon the mount of the congregation, in the sides of the north:

14 I will ascend above the heights of the clouds; I will be like the most High.

15 Yet thou shalt be brought down to hell, to the sides of the pit.

16 They that see thee shall narrowly look upon thee, and consider thee, saying, Is this the man that made the earth to tremble, that did shake kingdoms;

17 That made the world as a wilderness, and destroyed the cities thereof; that opened not the house of his prisoners?

18 All the kings of the nations, even all of them, lie in glory, every one in his own house.

Matthew 10:30

30 But the very hairs of your head are all numbered.

Matthew 25:41

41 Then shall he say also unto them on the left hand, Depart from me, ye cursed, into everlasting fire, prepared for the devil and his angels:

1 Peter 5:8

8 Be sober, be vigilant; because your adversary the devil, as a roaring lion, walketh about, seeking whom he may devour:

Philippians 2:5

5Let this mind be in you, which was also in Christ Jesus:

Psalms 24:1

The earth is the Lord's, and the fulness thereof; the world, and they that dwell therein.

Psalms 91:1

1 He that dwelleth in the secret place of the most High shall abide under the shadow of the Almighty.

Romans 6:3–7

3 Know ye not, that so many of us as were baptized into Jesus Christ were baptized into his death?

4 Therefore we are buried with him by baptism into death: that like as Christ was raised up from the dead by the glory of the Father, even so we also should walk in newness of life.

5 For if we have been planted together in the likeness of his death, we shall be also in the likeness of his resurrection:

6 Knowing this, that our old man is crucified with him, that the body of sin might be destroyed, that henceforth we should not serve sin.

7 For he that is dead is freed from sin.

Romans 8:35–39

35 Who shall separate us from the love of Christ? Shall tribulation, or distress, or persecution, or famine, or nakedness, or peril, or sword?

36 As it is written, For thy sake we are killed all the day long; we are accounted as sheep for the slaughter.

37 Nay, in all these things we are more than conquerors through him that loved us.

38 For I am persuaded, that neither death, nor life, nor angels, nor principalities, nor powers, nor things present, nor things to come,

39 Nor height, nor depth, nor any other creature, shall be able to separate us from the love of God, which is in Christ Jesus our Lord.

2 Timothy 3:16

16 All scripture is given by inspiration of God, and is profitable for doctrine, for reproof, for correction, for instruction in righteousness:

Bibliography

Blank, Wayne. "What Does Wicked Mean?" Daily Bible Study. editionDBSx201702et. http://www.keyway.ca/htm2010/20100921. htm (accessed September 20, 2019).

Church of the Great God (C.G.G.). 1992-2019. Bible Tools. "Greek/ Hebrew Definitions." https://www.bibletools.org/index.cfm/fuseaction/ Lexicon. show/ID/G4991/soteria.htm (accessed September 24, 2019)

Cole, Brendan. 2009. "What Did BOD Mean?" RTE Sport, February 27, 2009. https://web.archive.org/web/20090228234200/http:// www.rte.ie/ie/sportsixnations/entry/what_did_bod_mean (accessed September 23, 2019).

KJV Dictionary. 2019. "KJV Dictionary Definition: subtil." Website ©2019 AV1611.com. https://av1611.com/kjbp/kjv-dictionary/subtil. html (accessed September 20, 2019).

McGauran, Debbie. "The 6 Health Benefits of Laughter." Active Beat. QOOL Media and Concourse Media. 2019. https://www.activebeat. com/your-health/the-6-health-benefits-of-laughter/2/(accessed September 24, 2019).

Satan. Wikipedia, The Free Encyclopedia. https://en.wikipedia.org/w/ index.php?title=Satan&oldid=923237939 (accessed September 20, 2019).

Printed in the United States
By Bookmasters